Siegfried Gohr · Museum Ludwig Cologne

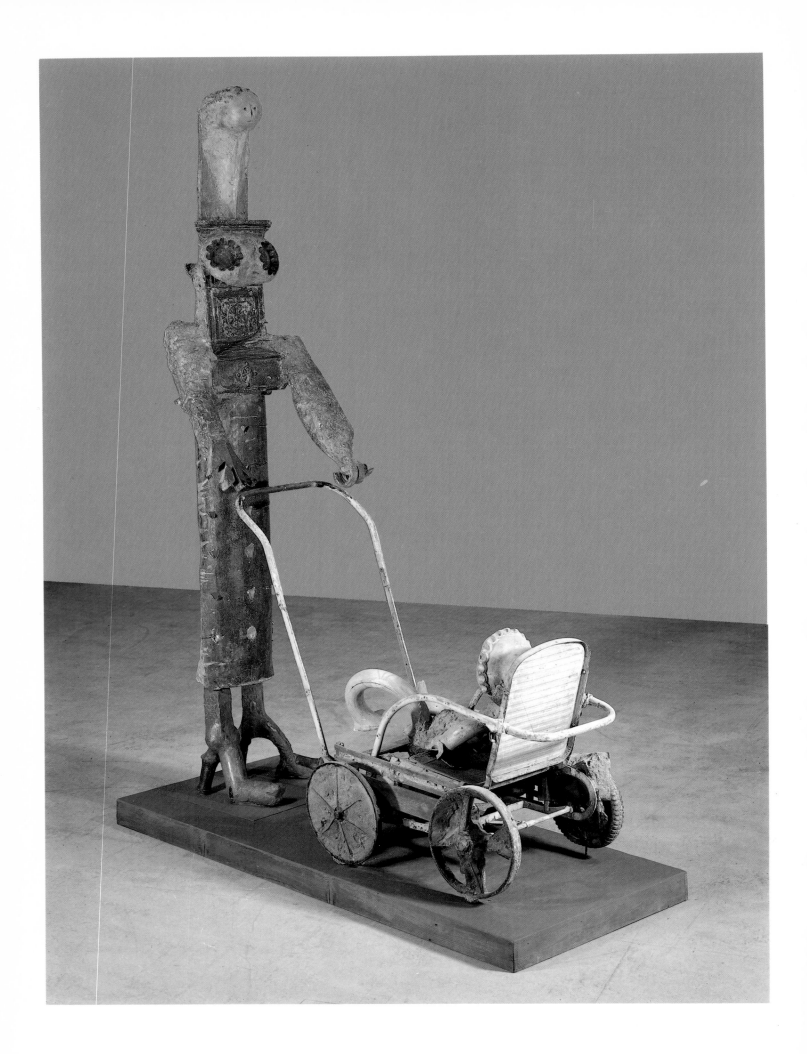

Siegfried Gohr

Museum Ludwig Cologne

Paintings, Sculptures, Environments
From Expressionism to the Present Day

Prestel-Verlag Munich

This book was published on the occasion of the opening of the new Museum Ludwig on 6 September 1986

Editing of the English edition: Michael Foster
Translation from the German: Mike Green
Designer: Dietmar Rautner

Photographs: Rheinisches Bildarchiv, Cologne

Jacket illustration: James Rosenquist, *Horse Blinders,* 1968-69 (detail, ill. 161)
Frontispiece: Pablo Picasso, *Woman with Pram,* 1950 (Photograph: Galerie Jan Krugier, Geneva)
© VG Bild-Kunst, Bonn 1986

Offset Lithography: Karl Dörfel Reproduktionsges. mbH, Munich
Typesetting: Fertigsatz GmbH, Munich
Printing and binding: Passavia Druckerei GmbH, Passau

Printed and bound in West Germany

Distribution in the USA and Canada by te Neues Publishing Company, 15 East 76 Street, New York, N. Y. 10021

Distribution in the UK, the Commonwealth (except Canada) and Ireland by Lund Humphries Publishers Ltd, 124 Wigmore Street, London W1H 9FE

ISBN 3-7913-0792-4 Plate volume in English
ISBN 3-7913-0790-8 Catalogue raisonné (German)
ISBN 3-7913-0791-6 Plate volume in English and Catalogue raisonné in case

ISBN 3-7913-0789-4 Plate volume in German
ISBN 3-7913-0771-1 Plate volume in German and Catalogue raisonné in case

Contents

The Museum Ludwig and Cologne as an Artistic Centre   7
From the Sonderbund Exhibition, 1912, to the New Museum, 1986

The Museum Ludwig and Cologne as an Artistic Centre

From the Sonderbund Exhibition, 1912, to the New Museum, 1986

The opening of the new building for the Museum Ludwig (art of the twentieth century) on 6 September 1986 marks the latest climax of Cologne's commitment to the art of this century. The new building has been erected on a plot of land between the cathedral, the Hohernzollern Bridge, the old city and the banks of the Rhine – in other words, on the very best site available. The history of Cologne from Roman times to the Middle Ages, and from the nineteenth century up to the present day, is all reflected in this focal point. The surrounding ensemble of buildings is a reminder of decisive eras in that history. Remains of the antique settlement recall the Roman founding-fathers of the city, and the medieval golden age is symbolized by its crowning glory, the cathedral, the foundation stone of which was laid in 1248. The cathedral also points to the time of its completion, after a break of centuries, in 1880. This was the period of Historicism, and the Hohernzollern Bridge and the railway station built during it stand not only as visible monuments to the sovereign authority achieved by Protestant Prussia over the Catholic Rhineland, but also as a symbol of the medieval city's entry into the modern industrial age.

This heart of Cologne on the left bank of the Rhine has its counterpart in the exhibition centre erected on the opposite side of the river in the twenties, a complex which bears witness to the final connection of the two settlements to form a unified city. The additional bridges built over the Rhine as a result produced further architectural highlights – for example, the daring construction of the Severin Bridge.

Apart from the Museum Ludwig, the new complex houses the contents of the Wallraf-Richartz Museum (art from 1300 to 1900), the Philharmonie (a concert hall seating 2,000), a film theatre and the art and museums' libraries. The completion of the building can be seen as the culmination of the many cultural and artistic undertakings which have occupied Cologne since the beginning of the nineteenth century. It was not until the sixties, however, that the city acquired its reputation as a centre of activity in modern art, an activity in which the Museum Ludwig is decisively involved as an institution and which is reflected in the decision to erect a new home for it. To some extent Cologne's development into a centre of modern art became possible only after the cultural shifts brought about by the division of Germany after the Second World War. The necessary realignment of cultural roles and opportunities among German cities gave Cologne the chance to create a climate receptive to modern art. Throughout this century there had been repeated efforts to keep abreast of international trends. The *Sonderbund* exhibition in 1912 represented an impressive beginning and served the organizer and artist, Walt Kuhn, as a prototype for his Armory Show in New York the following year. August Macke and the Rhineland Expressionists, as well as Max Ernst and the Dadaists after the First World War, all started to explore the international language of modern art being created in Paris. Between the wars, the situation became more stable, enabling Cologne to make its own contribution in the form of a constructive, socially committed figurative art. Headed by Franz Wilhelm Seiwert and Heinrich Hoerle, its various exponents were referred to collectively as the *Kölner Progressive* ('Cologne Progressives'). Although they never stayed in Cologne for any length of time,

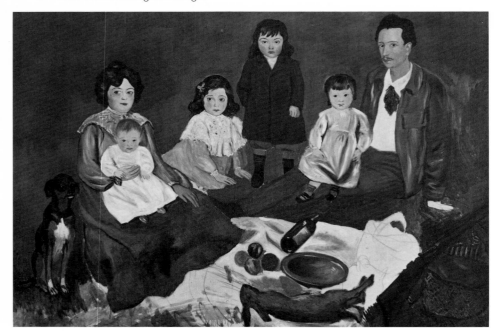

artists from other cities and countries, like Robert Delaunay, Hans Arp and Otto Freundlich, were constantly involved in the movements that followed Rhineland Expressionism and Dada.

Even before the Great War, and then consistently in the twenties, the Cologne museum built up a notable collection of modern art which, however, fell victim to the 'degenerate art' campaign carried out by the Nazis throughout Germany in 1937. Among the forty-five pictures confiscated were such masterpieces of modern art as Gauguin's *Riders on the Beach of Tahiti, Portrait of a Young Man* by Vincent van Gogh, *Field* by Edvard Munch, *The Soler Family* by Pablo Picasso, *Landscape: A View of Cannes* by André Derain, *Park Landscape: The Bosket (Town Square in Dresden-Neustadt)* by Ernst Ludwig Kirchner, Oskar Kokoschka's *Dents du Midi* and *Portrait of the actor Etlinger,* Franz Marc's *Horse in a Landscape, The Artist's Parents* by Otto Dix and Max Beckmann's *View of Blue Sea.*

It was a stroke of luck for the history of Cologne's museums that, as early as 1946, an important collection of modern art was presented to the city by the local lawyer, Dr. Josef Haubrich, who also assisted in its subsequent enlargement. Major Expressionist works came into the possession of the museum in this way, thus allowing Cologne to pick up the threads of its pre-war position at an unexpectedly rapid pace. More examples of international modern art were acquired during the following years – in 1958, for instance, through the purchase of the Willy Strecker collection, which included valuable works by Picasso, Matisse, Maillol, Kokoschka and Klee. Further representative works by classic modern artists were added to the collection as a result of the funds accruing from the Museum Jubilee Appeal, which was organized by Gert von der Osten in 1961. In that year the museum celebrated the 150th anniversary of its foundation by the professor and canon, Ferdinand Franz Wallraf. Von der Osten succeeded in putting together a sum of some four million marks from private, municipal and state sources. When the Jubilee gifts went on show in the anniversary exhibition, the public was able to admire masterpieces by Monet, Pissarro, Gauguin, Degas, Vuillard and Kirchner. Parallel to these successes of the museum's acquisitions policy, a lively artistic scene developed in the city, not least inspired by the efforts of its director of cultural affairs, Kurt Hackenberg. As in the period after the First World War, links were forged with Paris. The first post-war artists orientated themselves almost as a matter of course on the painting of the Ecole de Paris, as is reflected in the last purchases made by Dr. Haubrich. After 1960 the direction changed with the arrival of a new avant-garde belonging to the international Fluxus movement. Electronic music, visual arts, the new forms 'action' and

Oskar Kokoschka,
Dents du Midi

'happening', experimental theatre and literature – all met in a climate of mutual exchange and inspiration. Connections were formed with the Nouveau Réalisme of Paris, while some American artists – among them, John Cage and Christo – came to work in Cologne. The city's transformation into a centre of contemporary art had thus begun already at the outset of the sixties, even if was at first encouraged and defended by only a few enthusiasts.

In another field, that of the art trade and the galleries supporting the latest developments in art, there took place in 1967 an event which was to have far-reaching consequences – the first art market in the medieval assembly and concert hall of Gürzenich. Having grown into an internationally respected institution, the market is now held annually at the exhibition centre on the right bank of the Rhine. From the beginning, the

Otto Dix, *The Artist's Parents*

programme of the galleries involved has provided an excellent survey of the international art scene and, above all, has been responsible for making American art of the sixties known in Europe. The display of the Hahn collection in 1968 connected the museum for the first time with international currents.

The decisive moment for the future of the modern art collection in Cologne came in 1969. On 27 February of that year the museum opened its first display of the collection of Peter and Irene Ludwig. The couple from Aachen had offered the museum their important collection of new art on permanent loan. The leading New York artists, including Jasper Johns, Robert Rauschenberg, Roy Lichtenstein, Claes Oldenburg, Andy Warhol and George Segal, were as well-represented as artists of the European avant-garde, like Beuys, Yves Klein, Arman, Baselitz and Penck. The exhibition attracted 200,000 visitors – an exceptional success.

Under the influence of this event, things started to happen on the museum front, especially as the Ludwigs continually added new works to their original loan. Those responsible for the cultural policy of the city began to warm to the idea of a new museum building, an idea which had been aired from time to time in previous years. In the same year of 1969 a commission was formed to look into the relevant criteria and conditions. On 1 October 1975 a competition on a national basis was announced, with a number of foreign architects also being invited to participate. After various sites in the city had been considered, a decision was reached in favour of the prominent one behind the Cathedral. In the process of building the new museum the area between the cathedral and the river, which had been rather neglected since the war, was to be completely re-modelled.

On 5 February 1976 the city council voted unanimously for a deed of donation to be drawn up with the Ludwigs. It was agreed that Peter and Irene Ludwig should donate 350 modern works of art to the city of Cologne and that, in return, the city would found a Museum Ludwig to house both the donation and all works dating from after 1900 in the modern section of the Wallraf-Richartz Museum. The new Wallraf-Richartz Museum contains works from the Middle Ages up to 1900.

Thanks to the generous patronage of the Ludwigs, Cologne's cultural life was enriched by a new museum, one which has developed dynamically and expanded its collection considerably since 1976. Cologne's tradition of naming its museums after great patrons of the arts, and thereby honouring their involvement in the cultural affairs of the city, was upheld as the Ludwig Collection became the Museum Ludwig.

Besides Haubrich and Ludwig, numerous other donors have contributed to the quality and scope of the collections. An impressive series of paintings by Max Beckmann was bequeathed to the museum by Georg and Lilly von Schnitzler in 1957, although the works – among them, *Self-portrait with Black Beret* (1934) and the complex figure painting *The Organ-grinder* (1935) – could not be shown to the public for the first time until 1979. While this enrichment of the collection further accentuated its emphasis on Expressionism, the donation of Günther and Carola Peill in 1978 brought with it a beautiful and representative selection of the work of Ernst Wilhelm Nay, who lived in Cologne from 1951 until his death in 1968. Together with further important paintings, ranging from Max Ernst to Beckmann, this donation is especially rich in first-class water-colours and drawings.

If such past acts of patronage so obviously and generously benefit a particular museum, as has been the case with Haubrich's and Ludwig's in post-war Cologne, then their repercussions may be even more far-reaching than usual. They provide encouragement, and a challenge, to new generations of collectors and patrons. Thus, the future promises further donations, not only in the field of Expressionist art (focusing on Ernst Barlach), but also in that of contemporary German and American art. Cooperative projects are emerging in an open climate of discussion and mutual trust.

In Cologne, the concerns of museum policy, and of the artistic scene associated

with it, have always found expression in large-scale exhibitions surveying particular developments. Thus, major shows devoted to contemporary themes – for example, 'Happening and Fluxus' (1969), 'Now – The Arts in Germany' (1970) and 'Project '74' (1974) – have taken place at the Kunsthalle since it opened its doors in 1967. Finally, 1981 saw the ambitious exhibition 'Westkunst', held in the exhibition centre on the other side of the Rhine. These events opened up prospects for enlarging the museum's collection. This had, in fact, become possible with the first permanent loans from the Ludwigs, but the opportunities were not fully grasped at the time.

Ever since the mid-sixties Cologne and the Rhineland have been a favourite meeting ground for European and American avant-garde art. The two have been compared, sometimes resulting in heated debates on artistic approaches and concepts. These reflect, not least, the political history of East-West relations; for art, even if it avoids making overtly political statements in its form or content, cannot remain untouched by political, social and cultural events without losing its truthfulness. In retrospect, 'Project '74' can be seen to have contained the principle which has guided the policy of the museum for some years now – namely, the unbiased analysis and assessment of both European and American art. Today, it can be maintained that, since the appearance of the New York school of Abstract Expressionism, the history of art on these continents has split into two streams, that two different traditions have emerged. Again and again they come into close contact with each other but, in the final analysis, they retain two varying notions of what constitutes an 'image'.

This is the subject of the first exhibition in the new museum. Under the title 'Europe/America – The History of an Artistic Fascination since 1940' it investigates and presents the interactions and dynamic structure of this epoch. The exhibition has been planned as a demonstration on a temporary basis of the concept underlying the museum, bringing together an exceptional selection of work from the best post-war artists on both sides of the Atlantic. This concept will continue to constitute the museum's attractiveness and effectiveness, providing the criteria both for future exhibi-

tions and for the enlargement of the permanent collection. The willingness to cooperate, and the expectations connected with it, are equally great on the other side of the ocean.

The Museum Ludwig thus represents a rich treasure-store, and a mirror, of the art of the twentieth century. It has been possible to strengthen the collection of German Expressionism with first-class sculptures, while western visitors to the museum will be astounded at the abundance and variety of works of the Russian avant-garde. Max Ernst, Dada and Surrealism form a further focal point, one recalling the historical importance of the Cologne art scene after 1919. A whole room of the new museum is devoted to Picasso, the genius of the century, whose work from the forties onwards, and especially his sculptures, have attracted increased attention in recent years. The 'second avant-garde' of American and European art since 1945 is represented by series of important works which bear impressive witness to the revolutionary spirit and to the quite explosive creative atmosphere of the years 1955 to 1965, as a previously inconceivable Western Art established itself between Berlin, Cologne, Paris, London, Milan and New York. In that decade an important new German art began to emerge, its rise being continued today by a large number of artists.

The plates of the present volume allow the reader to experience the highlights of this comprehensive collection. On top of this, they provide an introduction to the exciting story of twentieth-century art, an art which has registered the upheavals of the era with seismographic exactitude and yet has presented that era with works which, for validity and seriousness of purpose, need not fear comparison with those of earlier times.

The eleven sections of this book correspond to the order of the rooms and their themes in the newly opened museum, thus allowing the reader to experience the richness of the collection in an imaginary tour of the building. The result is a panorama of the most significant achievements of modern art.*

*A second volume, its commentaries and black-and-white illustrations documenting the complete holdings of the museum with scientific thoroughness, is available in German.

Expressionism and Neue Sachlichkeit

The term 'Expressionism' had already been applied, before the First World War, to that art which appeared to explode the world of visible reality through abstraction, distortion or commitment to non-representational themes. Initially, it served as a generalizing label, a synonym for all new art which was articulating both the feeling of political crisis in Europe and the radical philosophical, scientific and artistic changes of the time.

After an interval of more than two generations since those revolutionary times on the eve of the Great War, the term's usage has been clarified. Although Expressionist tendencies were a part of the emergence of modern art in many European countries, and also of the American avant-garde of this century, nowadays 'Expressionism', often amended to 'German Expressionism', is applied to a movement which appeared in Dresden, Berlin, Munich and, in a different form, in the Rhineland. The revolution embodied in such groups of artists as the *Brücke* ('Bridge'), *Der Blaue Reiter* ('The Blue Rider'), *Der Sturm* ('The Storm') and the Rhineland circle of August Macke is characterized less by unity of style than by a rejection of the academic art prevailing in the Germany of Wilhelm II. A number of important contributions were also made by artists outside these groups.

The great achievement of the Brücke lay in the liberation of colour from the conventions that governed its use in landscape or in the outdated history painting of an Anton von Werner. It is significant that this new departure did not take place in the capital, Berlin, but in Dresden, and among artists who had got to know each other, not at the Academy of Art, but while studying architecture. Work together, whether in life painting or in portraying the countryside around Dresden, and the direct exchange of ideas and artistic discoveries were as much a part of everyday life in the Brücke as the recruitment of new members, the production of 'annual portfolios' and the organization of exhibitions. Outward circumstances and the increasingly individual development of the artists rendered such close collaboration in art and life impossible after 1910. With the first moves to Berlin, the varying interests and temperaments within the group became quite clear. They led to the break-up of the Brücke in 1913.

The group had progressed from the flickering impasto of the 'Monumental Impressionism' of 1907, as represented by Nolde's *Yellow and Red Roses,* to pictures largely constructed from flat areas of colour, as seen in Pechstein's *The Green Sofa* (1910) and Heckel's *Hunting Lodge near Moritzburg* (1910). Embracing the big-city environment of Berlin, Kirchner and Heckel changed not only the subject matter, but also the formal means and mood of their pictures. The barrenness and melancholy of the city set the tone in *Canal in Berlin* by Heckel. In *Female Half-length Nude with Hat* (1911) and *Five Women in the Street* (1913) Kirchner treated the demi-monde and the street respectively as significant elements of the city. Otto Mueller first became a member of the group in Berlin, but hardly changed either the subjects of his work, drawn from the world of gypsies and their life of ease, or his restrained use of colour, achieved by means of distemper.

After the First World War, the artists found themselves in a completely new personal and political situation. Schmidt-Rottluff kept closest to the ideal of unbroken, radiant colour, as can be recognized from a comparison between his *Still Life with Negro Sculpture* from the last year of the Brücke's existence, 1913, and another still life, *Delphinium in the Window,* of 1922. In his Swiss landscapes, Kirchner developed a monumental use of colour which absorbed the graphic elements from his works created during the years in Berlin. Following his tour of Germany in 1925-26, he painted the large-scale picture, *A Group of Artists,* which, with its portraits of Schmidt-Rottluff, Heckel, Mueller und himself, is like a memorial to the Brücke. Nolde, after his short period of contact with the younger artists, remained a lone wolf who, in his landscapes and especially in his religious works, arrived at ecstatic colour harmonies, along with apparently naive brushwork and a primitivistic figure style. The close ties to the landscape of northern Germany, which are so typical of Nolde, also left their mark on the work of other artists and groups. Paula Modersohn-Becker remained attached to the landscape, and to the artists' colony, of Worpswede despite the impressions she had gained earlier on in Paris, while Christian Rohlfs became enchanted with the medieval Westphalian town of Soest. The work of Ernst Barlach – another artist closely bound to north Germany – bears witness to a religious struggle which, although expressed in an imagery less overtly Christian than Nolde's, quite clearly possesses an existential dimension, even in such genre-like sculptures as *The Old Woman*.

The other significant sculptor of the Expressionist movement, Wilhelm Lehmbruck, cannot be compared in stylistic terms either with Barlach or with the painter-sculptors Kirchner, Heckel, Schmidt-Rottluff and Hermann Scherer, Kirchner's Swiss pupil. Lehmbruck worked in Rodin's studio in Paris, came into contact with Maillol's work and finally arrived at his expressive style in 1910-11, while still in Paris. His works were recognized early on, both in Europe and in America, as important sculptural achievements. *Female Torso* of 1910 and *Head of a Youth* of 1913 provide evidence of his consistent development during the decisive years: the rounded volumes of the torso are still reminiscent of Maillol, while the extended proportions of the head already betray his personal style. His sense of tectonics, noticeable even in details, the concentration on the emotional yet restrained, inward gesture, and the indefinable reaction to the surroundings expressed in the inclination of the head are elements which reveal Lehmbruck's greatness as a sculptor.

Together with Berlin, the other centres of Expressionism before the First World War – Munich and the Rhineland – were connected to each other not only by personal contacts and friendships, such as that between August Macke and Franz Marc, but also by joint participation in exhibitions. Open to other traditions than those embraced by the Brücke, Der Blaue Reiter came into being as a result of an intensive exchange of ideas between Wassily Kandinsky and Franz Marc. It was both a programme and an association of artists, and in the almanac which the two artists published in 1912, and which gave the group its name, Kandinsky provided a theoretical explanation of abstract art. The *Neue Münchner Künstlervereinigung* ('New Munich Association of Artists'), the forerunner of Der Blaue Reiter, had shown art from France (Picasso, Delaunay, Rouault and Braque) as well as from Russia (Larionov, Malevich, Goncharova and Burliuk) in its exhibitions: the exchange of artistic ideas thus stretched beyond national boundaries at a very early stage. The Blaue Reiter artists were less committed to a common goal than those of other groups. What they shared was a romantic way of thinking and feeling which included cosmological and synaesthetic notions. Various kinds of religious ideas permeate not only the work of Kandinsky and Marc, but also that of Klee.

August Macke was not interested in this spiritualism; he focused on the achievements of the Munich artists with regard to form and colour. His more secular view of art comprises elements derived from the Cubist treatment of volume, the pure colour of Delaunay and Marc as well as an attempt to go beyond nature in the use of colour harmonies. In spite of certain parallels with the work of Marc, his paintings contain nothing of the latter's mystical conception of nature. *Lady in a Green Jacket* (1913) and *Man Reading in the Park* (1914) are brillant examples of Macke's use of colour as a transmitter of light and of his purely formal approach towards pictorial harmony. By contrast, Franz Marc's pantheistic longing for harmony is directed at nature as such, which stands in perfect accord with itself without the presence of man. The painting *Wild Boars* (1913) exemplifies this attitude.

The shape of art in Germany changed dramatically after the First World War. The Bauhaus was established in 1919, Dada came into being in Berlin and Cologne, and *Neue Sachlichkeit* ('New Objectivity') and other forms of realism extended the spectrum of methods and styles. Max Beckmann, Oskar Kokoschka and Otto Dix created masterpieces in the twenties without forgetting the problems and experiences they had inherited from Expressionism. Following his mental and physical breakdown during the war, one of the first paintings that Max Beckmann produced in his new home of Frankfurt am Main in 1917 was *Landscape with Balloon*. The picture retains the intensity of the Expressionist view of life without, however, employing the vehement brushwork and discordant colours associated with the Brücke. In the course of the next years Beckmann came close to *peinture pure* but did not relinquish the searching treatment of mysterious subjects in his figure paintings. *Portrait of Reber,* from 1929, stands at the end of this period of confrontation with French art, while *The Organ-grinder* (1935) is representative of that series of hermetically symbolic pictures which had begun in 1932 with the triptych *Departure*. On hearing Hitler's speech at the opening of the 'degenerate art' exhibition on the radio in 1937, Beckmann went into voluntary exile in Holland.

After the war, when the artist was once more able to travel freely, he emigrated to America, where only a few more years of creative life remained to him. The powerful composition of *Woman with Mandolin in Yellow and Red* (1950) originated in the last year of his life and, in its use of strong local colours and the emphatic modelling of the figures, harks back to the mysterious pictures of the twenties.

Like Beckmann, Oskar Kokoschka became well-known in Paris during the inter-war years and he too went into exile (in England). But unlike Beckmann, he was able to produce a large body of late work, including triptychs, after the war. Kokoschka had left the Vienna of *Jugendstil* for Berlin, where he moved in the circles of Paul Cassirer and Herwarth Walden, owner of the gallery *Der Sturm* ('The Storm'). *Tilla Durieux* and *Peter Braun,* both originating in Berlin in 1910, exemplify the intense spiritual quality of the portraits by this painter who, in his poetry too, saw himself as a visionary. During the years in Dresden, from 1917 to 1924, Kokoschka's palette changed. Both in his portraits – for example, *The Heathens,* depicting Käthe Richter and Walter Hasenclever – and in his urban landscapes of Dresden, he developed an impasto application of glowing colours which excluded line, his most important artistic means before the war. Patches and islands of colour interlock and overlap like lumps of solid matter. They almost make a relief of the painted surface, which bears the traces of brush and palette-knife. At this time, Kokoschka was in close contact with Dresden intellectuals. It is only against the background of the old royal city, with its baroque flair, that Kokoschka's exuberant, sparkling colour becomes fully comprehensible. Dresden was not only important for him: the Brücke had its roots there, Otto Dix and Conrad Felixmüller were both natives of the city and George Grosz had studied there.

It was in Dresden and Berlin that Otto Dix produced the masterpieces of his minutely realistic painting style, using the glazing technique of the Old Masters. Around 1919, Dix had started painting powerfully dynamic Expressionist pictures in a Futurist vein. By the time he came to create *Portrait of Dr. Hans Koch* he had changed his style, but the inner restlessness and the horror of war are still there in these works from the first post-war years. In the merciless depiction of its subject, the portrait belongs among the artist's most impressive. Dix painted his *Portrait of the Poet Theodor Däubler* in 1927, the year he returned from Dresden to Berlin. Its old-fashioned style is reinforced by the choice of picture support: panel, as in the works of the early German masters.

Neue Sachlichkeit, to which parts of Dix's oeuvre may be ascribed, replaced Expressionism after 1920. Artists like Carlo Mense, Heinrich Davringhausen, Alexander Kanoldt and Georg Schrimpf met at times in Munich, as Mense's *Portrait of Davringhausen* indicates. Influences from new Italian art – de Chirico's circle and the periodical *Valori plastici* – became noticeable, and transformed these artists' socially committed realism into one of a genre-like, 'neoclassical' character. In the broadest sense, Carl Hofer's *Masquerade* of 1922 belongs to this development.

1 Ernst Ludwig Kirchner, *Female Half-length Nude with Hat*, 1911, 76 × 70 cm

2   Ernst Ludwig Kirchner, *Five Women in the Street*, 1913,   120 × 90 cm

3   Ernst Ludwig Kirchner, *A Group of Artists (The Painters of the Brücke)*, 1925/26, 168 × 126 cm

4   Ernst Ludwig Kirchner
The Railway Bridge, 1914
79 × 100 cm

5   Erich Heckel
Hunting Lodge
(Fasanenschlösschen)
near Moritzburg
1910, 97 × 120.5 cm

6   Erich Heckel, *Canal in Berlin*, 1912, 83 × 100 cm

7   Karl Schmidt-Rottluff, *Still Life with Negro Sculpture*, 1913, 73 × 68.5 cm

8   Karl Schmidt-Rottluff, *Delphinium in the Window*, 1922, 91 x 76 cm

9   Emil Nolde, *Visionaries,* 1916, 100.7 x 86.4 cm

10   Emil Nolde, *Young Woman and Men*, 1921, 101 × 73 cm

11   Emil Nolde, *The Bonnichsen Family*, c. 1915, 73.3 × 89 cm

12   Emil Nolde, *Yellow and Red Roses*, 1907, 64.5 × 83 cm

13 Max Pechstein, *The Green Sofa*, 1910, 96.5 x 96.5 cm

14   Otto Mueller, *Gipsy Hut with Goat*, c. 1925, 115.5 × 90 cm

15   Otto Mueller, *Two Gipsies with Cat*, c. 1926/27, 144.5 × 109.5 cm

16   Paula Modersohn-Becker
Worpswede Landscape, c. 1900
61.5 × 67.8 cm

17   Paula Modersohn-Becker
Still Life with Pumpkin, 1905
69.5 × 89.5 cm

18   Paula Modersohn-Becker
Self-portrait, 1906, 45.7 × 29.7 cm

19   Franz Marc, *Wild Boars*, 1913, 73.5 × 57.5 cm

20 August Macke, *Lady in a green Jacket*, 1913, 44 x 43.5 cm

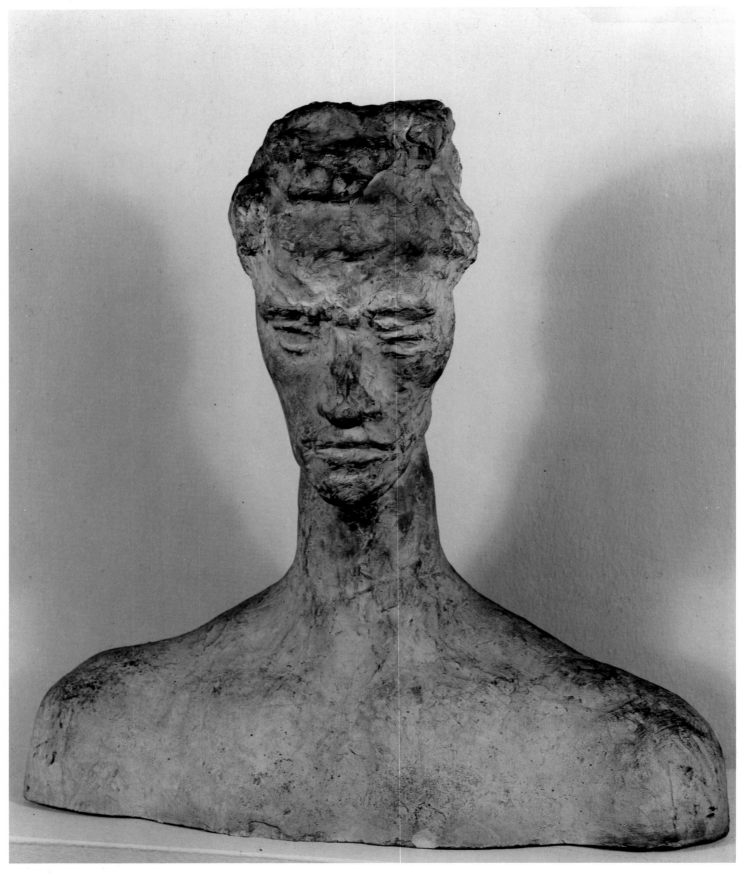

21   Wilhelm Lehmbruck
Head of a Youth, 1913, Height 46 cm

22   Wilhelm Lehmbruck
Female Torso, 1910, Height 115 cm

23   Oskar Kokoschka
Portrait of Tilla Durieux, 1910, 56 × 65 cm

24   Oskar Kokoschka
Portrait of Peter Baum, 1910, 65.5 × 47 cm

25   Oskar Kokoschka, *Dresden-Neustadt III,* 1921, 70 × 99 cm

26   Oskar Kokoschka, *The Heathens,* 1918, 75.5 × 126 cm

27   Max Beckmann
Portrait of Reber
1929, 140.5 × 72 cm

28   Max Beckmann *The Organ-grinder*, 1935, 175 × 120.5 cm

29   Max Beckmann, *Self-portrait with Black Beret,* 1934, 100 × 70 cm

30   Max Beckmann, *Beach*, 1935, 65.5 × 95.5 cm

31   Max Beckmann, *Woman with Mandolin in Yellow and Red*, 1950, 90 × 139 cm

32   Carlo Mense, *Portrait of H. M. Davringhausen*, 1922, 86.5 × 59.5 cm

33   Hermann Scherer, *Pair of Lovers*, 1924, Height 112 cm

34　Ernst Barlach, *Old Woman*, 1933, Height 56 cm

35   Otto Dix
Portrait of Dr. Hans Koch
1921, 100.5 × 90 cm

36   Otto Dix
Portrait of the Poet Theodor Däubler
1927, 150 × 100 cm

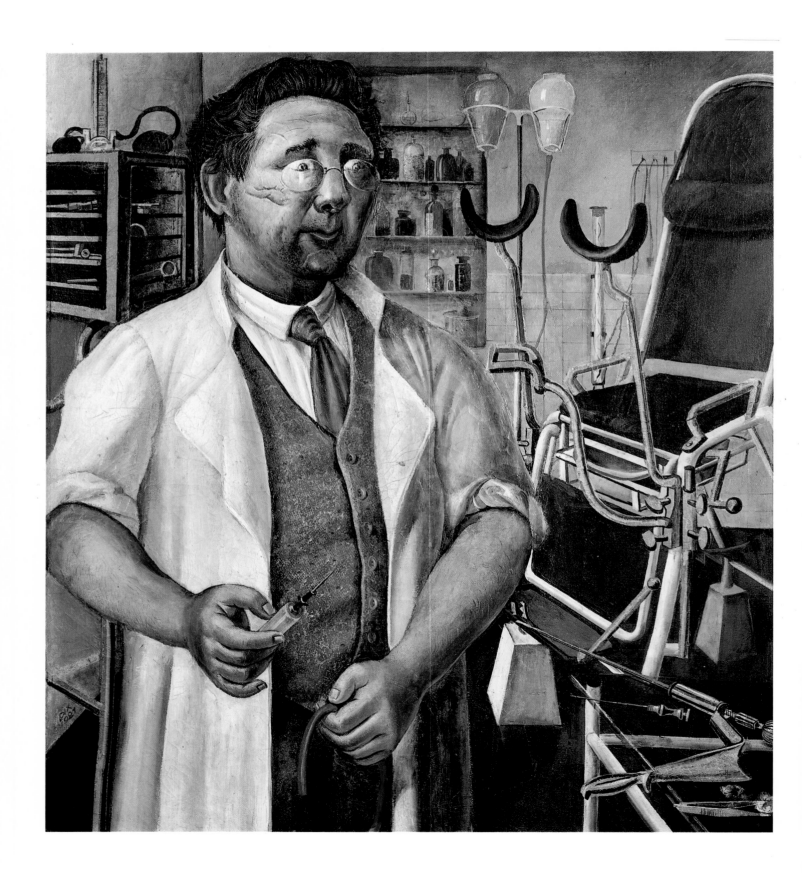

37   Gerhard Marcks, *Prometheus Bound II*, 1948, Height 78 cm

38   Ewald Mataré, *Grazing Horse,* c. 1930, Height 34 cm

39   Carl Hofer, *Masquerade*, 1922, 129 × 103 cm

2

Picasso and Classic Modern Art in France

The most significant consequence of the artistic conclusions which Picasso, Braque and Léger drew from their confrontation with the work of Cézanne in Paris in 1907 was the birth of Cubism. The effect on Braque of Picasso's *Demoiselles d'Avignon* – on which he was working in Paris during 1907 – and the resulting friendship and cooperation between the two, belong to the most fortunate and famous events in modern art. The discussion about the respective parts played by each of these painters in the creation of the new style, and hence about their relative historical importance, has flared up again in the wake of various exhibitions held in recent years. As a result, Braque's contribution has come to command greater attention and recognition. The revolutionary achievement of Cubism lay, on the one hand, in its abolition of central perspective as the direct or indirect means of defining pictorial space and, on the other, in the invention of collage. In addition, Picasso's Cubist sculptures have had an immeasurable effect on the art of the twentieth century. Cubist works, however, only rarely approach the degree of abstraction attained in paintings like Picasso's *Woman with a Mandolin* of 1910. Even here, the contours of the body, and of the instrument, can still be discerned among the structure of lines and grey-brown planes. The same is true of Braque's still life of 1912, *Glass, Violin and Sheet of Music*. The dissolution of the optical appearance of objects into facets, colours and textures, and the translation of volume and space into colour which forms 'corridors', or into staggered, splintered planes which interlock with one another, were recognized by Picasso and Braque as characteristics of a new art, as were the resultant clarity of objects' definition in space and the collapse of the duality between plane and volume. The components in these artists' compositions became steadily smaller, capturing ever more facets of the objects represented. In 1912-13 this development gave way to the subdued, clear rhythm of the collage, and that is the stage epitomized by the Cologne picture of Braque's, although the 'collage' elements have been rendered in paint.

Braque's and Picasso's works of the Cubist years are very closely related to each other, but they reveal, nevertheless, the difference in temperament and origins between the two artists. Picasso retains an underlying aggression in his work – apparent in the deliberate contrasts between groups of forms – whereas Braque respects the picture plane as a decorative and, as it were, inviolable continuum. This 'lyrical' approach is very much in the French tradition. Picasso, on the other hand, never completely denied the eruptive and the expressive, aspects of his work which are particularly dominant in 1907-08.

Henri Laurens acquired the Cubist formal vocabulary through his acquaintance with Braque, but subjected it to a personal interpretation in his collages and sculptures: *The Guitar* of 1914, for example, is closer to Picasso. Rich in associations, the work suggests the interplay of arching and hollow bodies by means of a collection of unfolding, interlocking planes only sparingly accentuated by colour. It is the plastic equivalent of a guitar: not confining itself to a simple description of the instrument, it conveys an image of it when vibrating with sound.

While Laurens followed Picasso with his three-dimensional constructions, Raymond Duchamp-Villon, the brother of Marcel Duchamp and Jacques Villon, drew different conclusions from the Cubist analysis of form. He belonged, together with his brothers, Léger, Gleizes, Metzinger and other Cubists, to the Group of Puteaux. The sculpture *Seated Woman*, of 1914, almost resembles a marionette with its simplified, rounded forms. In the complicated interlocking of its various masses one can, however, recognize an interest in the studies of motion found in Futurist sculpture, which, along with Cubist abstraction, was to form the essence of the artist's major work, *The Great Horse* of 1914.

At the very heart of the Cubist movement there stands a second Spanish painter, Juan Gris. Gertrude Stein, that committed witness of the creation of a new art in Paris, once said that Cubism was hardly conceivable without the melancholy and inexorability of Spain. Gris's work after 1914 subjects the visible world to a pictorial formula in the strictest mould of Synthetic Cubism. Iconographically, *Syphon, Glass and Newspaper* (1915) remains within the realm of such typical Cubist subjects as landscape and still life, but its pictorial construction points in other directions. Rather than taking apart the objects and analysing them, Gris recreates them from a synthesis of surface patterns. In doing so, he formulated the main elements of Purism, a movement of the twenties with which Fernand Léger was closely associated.

Léger had developed his own variant of Cubism under the influence of Picasso's works of 1908. Even in his mature Cubist works – which he called *Form Contrasts* – he remained true to the powerful, sculptural element in this early stage of Cubism. Based on his experiences with it in the years 1913-14, when he, like Delaunay, allowed colour to play a decisive part in his style, Léger developed an imagery of modern civilization. The painting *The Pink Tug* (1918) demonstrates his sober yet optimistic attitude, one which was to influence American art in the sixties. Some parts of Léger's pictures from 1918 retain the effect of shining metal from the earlier *Form Contrasts*. However, the vertical strips in the background of *The Pink Tug* already signalize the appearance of his new pictorial architecture.

It was not in Léger's work that the first signs of a development beyond Cubism became apparent. Picasso himself had already hinted at a surprising new turn in 1914 as he produced drawings in the style of Ingres. His reappraisal of the classical figure style had begun. *Woman in Green Dressing-gown* of 1922 alludes to antique sculpture in its head seen in profile and in its relief-like interpretation of a female body placed against a neutral, marble-coloured background. In spite of this voluminous neoclassicism, with its references to Antiquity, Picasso's classical style was more concerned with drawing, with the heritage of Ingres. In such works as *Harlequin with Folded Hands* he did away with the traditional relationship between drawing und colour: the precise graphic delineation of the motif contrasts and interacts with patches of colour arranged in an almost abstract fashion. The painter himself, not the motif, determines the organization of the various elements of the picture. As in Cubism, they are used in an autonomous way: classical subject matter was not to be equated with a return to pre-Cubist illusionism. Although it retains the guitar and fruit bowl of earlier years, the still life of 1925 also belongs within the group of classical works, as is indicated by its inclusion of an antique marble fist. It occupies a very special position among the still lifes created between 1922 und 1926 owing to its large-scale graphic design and the free use of colour.

In his own, unmistakable way, Picasso had shaped, or helped to shape, all the movements of modern art up to Surrealism. With *Guernica* he created, in 1937, the masterpiece of the politically committed art of his time. When the Museum of Modern Art in New York opened a large retrospective exhibition of his work on 15 November 1939, the artist was at the height of his fame.

In spite of the war and the occupation of Paris by the Germans, Picasso stayed in France and created, during these years, numerous urban landscapes, still lifes and pictures of women (mostly half-lengths) as well as sculptures. Without treating the horror and abominations of war explicitly, he nevertheless made the threat to existence visible in his work. The sculptures *Head of a Woman* of 1941, and particularly *Woman with Artichoke* of 1942, reveal the artist to be searching for ancient powers of defence against evil and fear. He invokes the image of woman as a benevolent goddess bringing salvation, a Madonna, or as an ominous bringer of death. Stylistic echoes of Cubism are unmistakable but, instead of employing them in his earlier analytical manner, the artist uses them as symbols of disintegration and the threat of destruction. The spirit of the post-war age – in Paris, the era of the Existentialists – is already forshadowed by Picasso in these wartime works.

The liberation in 1945 made it possible for him to travel again. Whereas he had often visited the French Atlantic coast in the inter-war years, he now preferred the Mediterranean, living for a time at Cape d'Antibes and later at Vallauris. Pictures of this southern landscape, and of family life too, appear about 1950. At the same time, Picasso increasingly turned his attention to the major works of earlier masters such als Manet, Velásquez and Rembrandt. It seems as though the more than seventy-year-old artist had begun to assess his position in the history of art. In the sixties, Picasso developed a tempestuous late style which is excellently represented in the Museum Ludwig by *Melon-eaters* (1967), *Reclining Woman with Bird* (1968) and *Musketeer with Cupid* (1969). The vehemence and vitality of these pictures from the last years of his life are astonishing, even if the occasional detail – such as the hollow-cheeked head in *Melon-eaters* – hints at the transitoriness of life. Presumably a self-portrait, *Man with Hat* of 1970 is a shattering vision of death, a pitiless confrontation with the End, rendered with a masterful economy of means reminiscent of Rembrandt.

Only during this century have the late works of great artists been experienced and analysed as a separate category. Apart from Picasso, both Léger and Matisse stand out by their production of quite distinctive conclusions to a life's work. The one developed a monumental figure style, while the other created a unique series of works with his cut-outs. The late work of both artists had a considerable effect on the art of the sixties, particularly in America.

Like many other European artists, Léger spent the duration of the war in New York. In this new environment he reformulated that optimism about civilization which had dominated his work in the twenties, affirming it in large-scale compositions that combine figurative and abstract elements. This group of works deals with themes from the world of the circus *(La grande Parade),* construction work *(Les Constructeurs)* and pleasurable amusement *(La partie de Campagne). The Country Excursion* of 1954 embodies all Léger's achievements after the Second World War. The forms are enclosed by strong contours and, in combination with large areas of mostly unbroken colour, radiate a serene and peaceful mood which raises an everyday situation to an event worthy of artistic treatment.

While Léger was affirming the earthly paradise of man within modern civilization, the Matisse of the late cut-outs excluded all references to the contemporary world. Since the illustrations to his book *Jazz,* and the decoration of the chapel in Vence, he had produced no more paintings, turning instead to the technique of collage in the form of cut-outs in coloured paper. A world of animals, flowers and women evokes paradise and the Golden Age. In these works, time disappears in an abstract experience of space. The simplicity of the means employed, and the total concentration on striking motifs, create a consummate surface rhythm, which Matisse fashions with regard to the grandeur of decorative art of the past. *Women and Apes* belongs to a group of large collages from the years 1952 and 1953 which seem to invoke the paradisiacal scenery of the South Seas. Mankind and nature are in harmony thanks to compositions of an almost heraldic boldness and impressiveness.

In their late works, these three great masters of the century – Picasso, Léger and Matisse – summed up their creative lives, and their conceptions of 'image' were to have far-reaching consequences. With his 'collage' sculptures of the fifties – *Woman with Pram,* for example – Picasso, as an ever-alert contemporary, took part in the reappraisal of the three-dimensional work of Dada and Surrealism. Finally, in his aggressively expressive late paintings he reacted in a similar way to the post–1960 situation as did younger artists at the close of the 'informal' movement. Although the self-portrait hardly occurs among the subjects of these years, Picasso, too, defined himself as an artist with these erotic and theatrically narrative pictures. Léger concluded his work as the pictorial architect he had been since Cubism. His pictorial world had changed, but his primary goal remained the depiction of a palpable reality which, in the manner of popular art, was immediately intelligible. By means of his cut-outs Matisse was able to intensify further that dream of lust for life and splendour of colour which had guided him since his first Fauvist works in 1905. In his hands, an apparently clumsy handicraft became a means of realizing artistic intentions with the utmost clarity, helping him to achieved monumentality in his large-scale wall decorations.

40   Henri Matisse, *Seated Girl*, c. 1909, 41.5 × 33.5 cm

41   Fernand Léger
The Pink Tug, 1918, 65.5 × 92 cm

42   Henri Laurens
The Guitar, 1914, Height 44 cm

43   Georges Braque, *Glass, Violin and Sheet of Music,* 1912, 64.5 × 91.5 cm

44 Juan Gris, *Syphon, Glass and Newspaper*, 1916, 55 × 46.5 cm

45   Pablo Picasso, *Head of a Picador*
with Broken Nose, c. 1901–03, Height 18.5 cm

46   Pablo Picasso
Woman with Mandoline, 1910, 91.5 × 59 cm

47   Pablo Picasso, *Harlequin with Folded Hands*, 1923, 129 x 96 cm

48   Pablo Picasso, *Woman in Green Dressing-gown*, 1922, 130.3 × 96.5 cm

49   Pablo Picasso, *Mandoline, Bowl of Fruit and Marble Fist*, 1925, 97.5 × 131 cm

50   Pablo Picasso, *Head of a Woman (Dora Maar)*, 1941, Height 80 cm

51   Pablo Picasso, *Ile de la Cité – View of Notre-Dame de Paris*, 1945, 80 × 120 cm

52   Pablo Picasso, *Woman with Artichoke*, 1942, 195 × 132 cm

53   Pablo Picasso, *Melon-eaters*, 1967, 114 × 146 cm

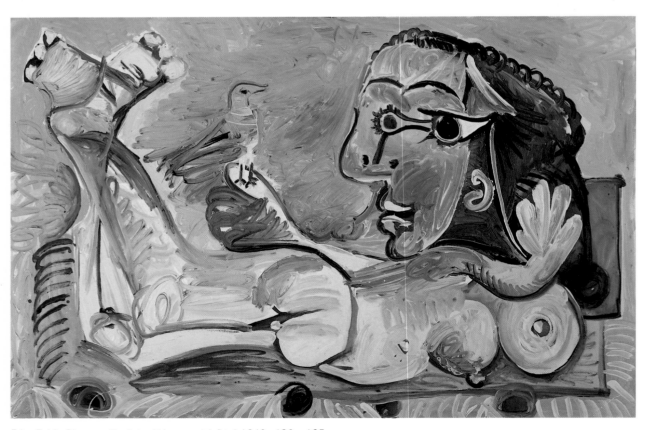

54   Pablo Picasso, *Reclining Woman with Bird*, 1968, 130 × 195 cm

55   Pablo Picasso, *Musketeer and Cupid*, 1969, 194.5 × 130 cm

56   Pablo Picasso, *Ruffled Dove*
1953, Height 20 cm

57   Pablo Picasso, *Portrait of a Man*
with Hat, 1970, 80 × 64.5 cm

58   Fernand Léger, *The Twins*, 1929/30, 73 × 92 cm

59   Fernand Léger, *The Country Excursion*, 1954, 194.5 x 194.5 cm

60   Henri Matisse, *Women and Apes*, 1952, 71.7 × 286.2 cm

61   Raymond Duchamp-Villon, *Seated Woman*, 1914, Height 73 cm

3

The Art of the Russian Avant-garde, the Blaue Reiter and the Futurists

Information about the history and achievements of Russian art in the first decades of this century rarely reached the artistic circles of the western world. Furthermore, very few works were in the possession of collections and museums outside Russia, so that knowledge of originals remained scant. The acquisition of a superb group of works by Kasimir Malevich by the Stedelijk Museum, Amsterdam in the 1950s represented the first step towards an assessment of the east European avant-garde which, in the course of the following years, developed to a point where a coherent picture of revolutionary Russian art emerged.

Contact between Russian artists and modern movements in western capital cities (especially Munich and Paris) had already intensified by the end of the last century. A large number of artists travelled to western Europe to complete their training, and some of them stayed on in Germany or France. For many years, Kandinsky, who, along with Chagall and others, was involved in the first exhibition of the *Blaue Reiter* ('Blue Rider') in Munich, acted as a relayer of information between the two avant-garde movements through his regular sojourns in both east and west.

In contrast to the avant-garde movements in western countries, Russian art before and after the revolution of 1917 was concerned not only with the fine arts but with all aspects of visual culture. The inclusion of film, photography, design, fashion, propaganda, theatre and architecture in one common movement reflected a social utopia of enormous dynamism and explosive force which, however, was to last only until the end of the twenties. For the first time, modern visual arts were deliberately employed in changing society. The social and artistic processes that had taken place gradually and systematically in France, for example, were accomplished in Russia in a single concentrated step. That atmosphere of change and upheaval which finally led to the October Revolution of 1917 was already noticeable at the end of the nineteenth century in, say, the writing of Tolstoy, Pasternak, Chlebnikoff and Mayakovsky.

In the field of painting, the approach of Kasimir Malevich was the most original and significant. Numerous artists had been fascinated by Cubism and Futurism, but with Suprematism Malevich created a wholly individual form of abstract art which was influenced to a considerable degree by the tradition of Russian icon painting. After an Impressionist phase, he painted such pictures as *Landscape* (1909) which deal with peasant life in rural Russia for the very first time. The broadly rhythmic composition of the picture and the powerful modelling of the objects in clear, unbroken colours betray the modernity of Malevich's art at this time. References to the visible world are still clearly defined, yet the surface rhythms give rise to a highly individual organization of layers of space which is without parallel in either western or eastern avant-garde styles. That Malevich was aiming at a new conception of pictorial space, rather than at an abstract arrangement of the picture plane, is demonstrated by such a mature example of his Suprematist style as *Dynamic Suprematism no. 57,* which he painted a few years later. Blocks and splinters of colour appear to be floating and expanding in a cosmic space, an impression achieved by imperceptible shifts and displacements in the proportions. Radiant, unbroken colours complete the link between Malevich's vision and the powerful spirit of the Revolution. He had developed his theory of modern art in numerous writings. Starting from 'supernaturalism', these theoretical considerations culminated in the notion of Suprematism, which sought the "supremacy of pure feeling in the visual arts". In a most impressive way, Malevich united and developed further the various traditions available to the Russian avant-garde. Influences from Fauvism in the use of colour and from Cubism and Futurism in the idea of dynamic pictorial space, as well as a reappraisal of Russian folk art, were things that many artists had in common, but Malevich pressed on towards a radically new form of picture, achieving it in his famous *Black Square* of 1913. From here, his path led him to an architectonic world based on the pure forms realized in his paintings. In the twenties he created a series of plaster models which, despite their tiny scale, generate an immense spatial power.

The Futurist influence, which was of only brief importance in Malevich's work, became the principle governing that of Mikhail Larionov and his wife Natalia Goncharova. Larionov developed it into a style he termed 'Rayonism', in which motifs dissolved into coloured bundles of line (rays, rayons). As early as 1911 this method gave birth to such abstract dynamic compositions as *Rayonism in Red and Blue (Beach)*. The crossing and interpenetrating rays of objects are the subject of the still life *Rayonist Sausages and Mackerels* of 1912. Like Larionov, Natalia Goncharova visited Paris at an early stage and took part in exhibitions of the Russian avant-garde in various western cities. In her painting she adopted, as did Larionov, elements of motion deriving from Cubism and Futurism, but also included reminiscences of Russian icons as well as the vivid colours and plastic forms of folk art.

The possibilities of the Cubo-Futurist style were translated into powerful works by two women artists, Alexandra Exter and Ljubov Popova. The former transformed Cubism's faceting of objects into a play of forms which, suffused with radiant light, possesses a lyrical character somewhat reminiscent of Feininger's landscapes. Popova worked her way through all the styles of the Russian avant-garde. From Expressionist beginnings, she progressed to a most individual treatment of Cubism – as witnessed by the powerful *Relief* of 1915 – and finally approached the spatial conception of Malevich's Suprematism. This last phase in her work is embodied in the painting *Painterly Architectonics,* produced in 1920 and bereft of all figurative associations. Irregular fragments are placed in relation to a seemingly curved area in the middle in such a way as to evoke the impression of movement in space.

While Popova was finding her own way towards more or less Suprematist compositions around 1920, some of Malevich's students were adapting it more directly – Nikolai Suetin, for example, in his *Composition* of about 1922-23. A personal, gentle rhythm of form, together with a restrained use of delicate shades of colour, distinguish Suetin's artistic temperament from that of his teacher. In the years around 1920, as Malevich himself was reaching the conclusion of his work in painting and turning to architectural design instead, Alexander Rodchenko had arrived at a similarly extreme position with his group of black pictures. *Black on Black* of 1918 formulates the demise of the 'picture' in a manner as radical as Malevich's *Black Square.* Only the geometric forms, placed like internal drawing on the black background, allow painting to become at all visible. Such works could not but lead to activity in other areas of the visual arts. Not until the American abstract art of an Ad Reinhardt was black to be treated in a similar way.

The opposite pole of Russian Constructivism's strict tectonics was inspiration through native folk art. Marc Chagall enriched this subject matter by including in it the imaginative world of images from Russian ghettoes. At an early stage, his teacher, Leon Bakst, drew his attention to modern French art, which he eventually got to know at first hand during a lengthy first stay in Paris. In particular, Van Gogh and Gauguin left their mark on his use of colour, the individuality of which is apparent in *Sabbath,* painted in the French capital in 1910. The glowing intensity of primary colours conjures up the motionless, almost stifling stillness of the day of rest, when time passes with a deadening slowness. Chagall was never to relinquish such memories of his childhood, and they remained the source of his fantasies throughout a very long life. Similarly, colour always formed the basis of his art, despite an early use of Cubist means. The floating, almost flying arrangement of objects in space and the leitmotiv of the hovering figure provide a dreamily narrative contrast to the spatial dynamics of Constructivism. At the beginning of his creative life Chagall created from his pre-Surrealist world of fables a thoroughly modern style of composition which, in his late work, dissolved into flowing constellations of great decorative force. To these latter belongs the large-scale picture *Moses Breaking the Tablets of the Law* of 1955-56, which was originally intended for a church at Vence in southern France. Chagall's life and work exemplify the close links between Russian and French art. A decisive part in the forging of these links had been played by Kandinsky, despite the fact that he worked for many years in Germany.

Even before the beginnings of modern art, Munich had acquired a certain fascination for those Russian artists who travelled to western Europe. It is, therefore, hardly surprising that Russian painters were involved in the foundation of the Blaue Reiter in 1910-11. Besides Kandinsky, who created the great pioneering works, Alexej Jawlensky also worked in Munich, and a large number of other Russian artists participated in the Blaue Reiter exhibitions.

The road to abstraction, which Kandinsky had marked out with painting of an immateriality comparable to that of music, was trodden by relatively few artists at that time. The effect of Kandinsky's early abstract style, which had not yet undergone the geometric hardening of the Bauhaus years, was not to be felt until the advent of Abstract Expressionism in America. *The White Stroke* of 1920 combines elements from his floating cosmos of coloured space with hints of the geometric abstraction of subsequent years. Jawlensky's style, on the other hand, remained indebted for a long time to the bold colour of folk art and to Fauvism's emphasis on the picture plane. Subjects such as *Still Life with Vase and Jug* still dominated his work in 1937, even if his compositions had become more restrained.

The Russian avant-garde is also characterized by a continual occupation with the art of the Italian Futurists. Early Futurist contacts with Munich and with the group surrounding Herbert Walden's Sturm Gallery in Berlin meant that Futurism's optimism and infectious energy were transmitted to Germany as well. Apart from Marinetti, it was, among others, Boccioni, Severini and Balla who rigorously reinterpreted the forms of Cubism for their own purposes which, as with the Russians, included the realization of social goals and utopias.

62   Kasimir Malevich, *Suprematist Architecton*, c. 1926, Height 6.5 cm

65   Michail Larionov, *Rayonist Sausages and Mackerels*, 1912, 46 × 61 cm

66   Michail Larionov, *Rayonism in Red and Blue (Beach)*, 1911, 68 × 52 cm

67   Natalia Goncharova, *Portrait of Larionov*, 1913, 105 × 78 cm

68   Alexandra Exter, *Cubo-Futurist Composition (Port)*, c. 1912 - 14, 129 x 200 cm

69   Alexandra Exter
Colour Dynamics, 1916/17,
89.5 × 54 cm

70   Ljubov Popova, *Painterly Architectonics*, c. 1920, 57.5 x 44 cm

71 Ljubov Popova, *Relief,* 1915, 66.3 × 48.5 cm

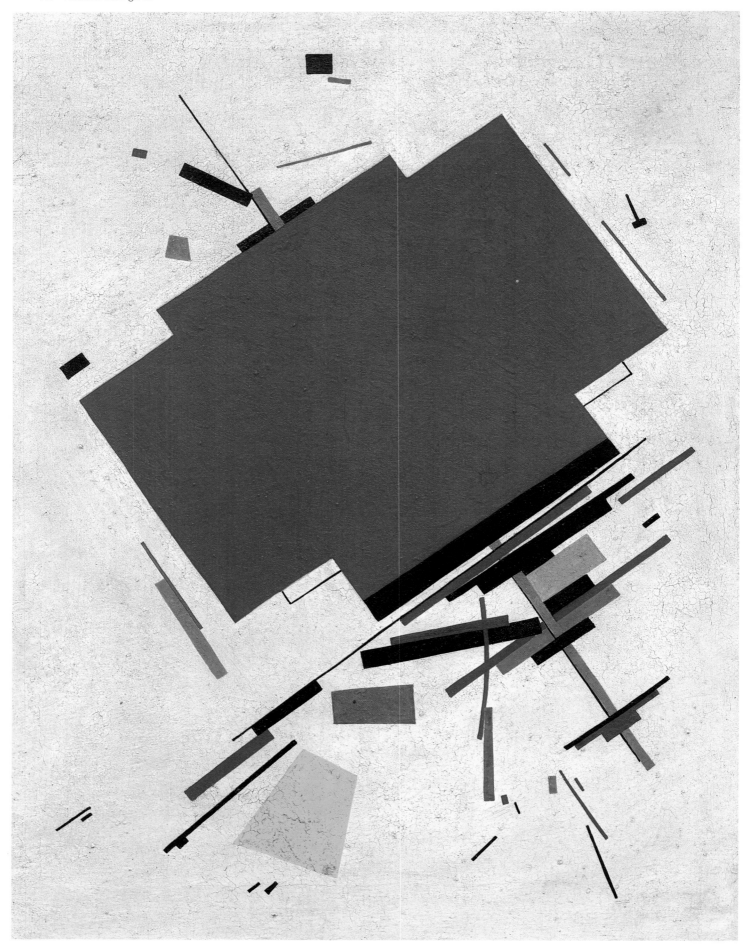

72   Nikolai Suetin, *Composition*, c. 1922/23, 65 × 48 cm

73   Alexander Rodchenko, *Black on Black,* 1918, 105 × 70.5 cm

74   Marc Chagall
Sabbath, 1910, 90.5 × 94.54 cm

75   Marc Chagall
Moses Breaking the Tablets of the Law,
1955, 228 × 154 cm

76   Alexej von Jawlensky, *Still Life with Vase and Jug*, 1909, 49.5 x 43.5 cm

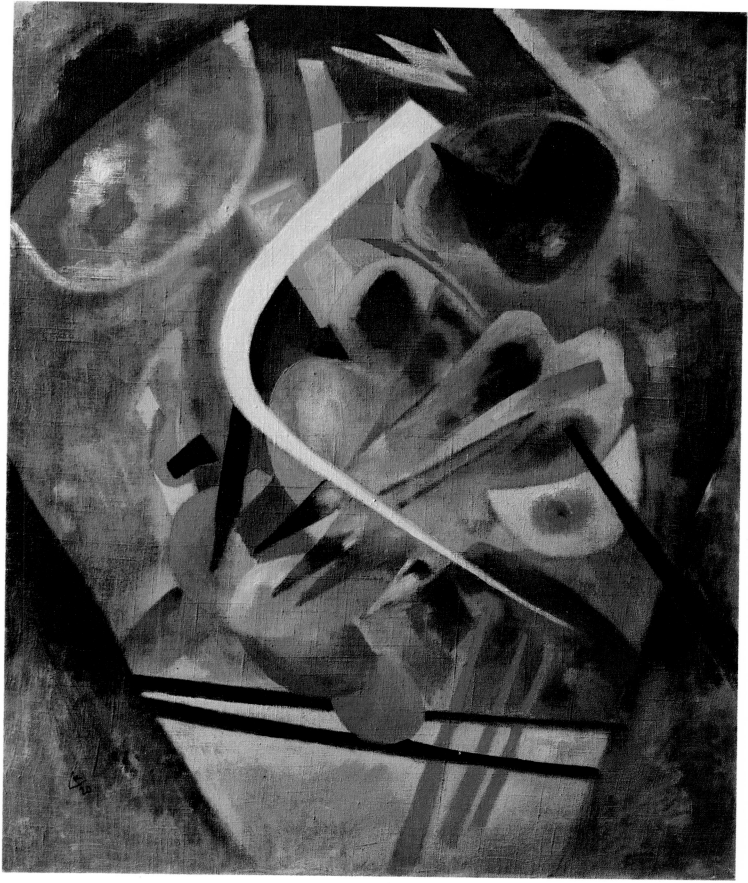

77   Wassily Kandinsky, *The White Stroke*, 1920, 98 × 80 cm

78   Gino Severini, *Collage*
c. 1912-15, 51 x 61 cm

79   Mario Sironi, *Yellow Aeroplane*
with Urban Landscape
1915, 71 x 53 cm

80 Antoine Pevsner, *Dernier Élan*, 1961/62, Height 66.8 cm

4

Constructive Tendencies:
From the Bauhaus to Abstraction-Création

The founding of the Bauhaus by Walter Gropius in Weimar in 1915, the formation of De Stijl by a group of Dutch artists that included Theo van Doesburg and Piet Mondrian in Leyden in 1917, the art of the Russian avant-garde before and after the October Revolution in 1917, and the activities of L'Esprit Nouveau centred around Léger, Le Corbusier and Ozenfant in Paris – these were the most important stages in the early history of constructivist art. In spite of great differences in style, these groups pursued the common goal of a rational organization of life in modern society. It was artists who formulated most clearly the hope for a radical reformation in cultural and political life after the old Europe had collapsed with the First World War. They extended their activities to include architecture, town planning, design, film-making and photography. The Bauhaus looked to bring all forms of art together in creative cooperation, taking its example from the workshops involved in the building of medieval cathedrals. Mastery of craftsmanship, as well as the theoretical and practical understanding of the principles governing each art form, were the aims of teaching at the Bauhaus, which included initially the idea of a *Gesamtkunstwerk* ('total work of art') as German Romanticism had conceived it. Similarly, the organized association of artists with the aim, on the one hand, of overcoming the isolation of art within society and, on the other, of actively employing art in a constructive way on all levels of that society derived from the aesthetics of German Idealism. Gropius's vision fascinated a very wide range of artists, inducing people of quite opposing temperaments to work together, at least for a time, to realize the common goal – people like Paul Klee, Oskar Schlemmer, Lyonel Feininger, László Moholy-Nagy, Wassily Kandinsky, Gerhard Marcks, Josef Albers and many others. The move from Weimar to Dessau in 1925, the increasing influence of the Russian Constructivists and the emphasis of Bauhaus teaching on practical application led, under Gropius's successor, the architect Hanns Meyer, to a serious limitation of the scope for that 'free art' which had played such an important part in the founder's original concept. At the same time, however, the international repercussions of Bauhaus aesthetics were on the increase and, following its move to Berlin and its eventual closure in 1932, Mies van der Rohe's New Bauhaus continued to exert significant influence from its home in Chicago.

The Constructivism of the twenties was the last avant-garde movement which united East and West before the political changes in Germany, Italy and Russia caused a radical break in the continuity of the history of art. With the international 'Pressa' exhibition in Cologne in 1928, a united avant-garde came together for the last time in a large-scale show.

The aesthetic demands of the Constructivists represented a radical challenge to the concept of 'image' which had governed western art up to that time. The autonomy of the image in relation to nature was so complete that, by 1930, Theo van Doesburg was using the term 'concrete picture'. Works of art had rid themselves both of comparability with nature and of the control exercised by the subjectivity of the artist. Visible reality and personal communication on the part of the artist had still been in evidence in Cubism and the abstraction of Der Blaue Reiter. Mondrian completely abandoned such attachments. In *Tableau I* of 1921 he orders the surface of the picture according to a harmony of vertical and horizontal lines, inserting between them squares or rectangles in the primary colours blue, red and yellow. The paint bears no traces of its application, is smooth and impersonal. The same is true of Moholy-Nagy's *On a White Ground* (1923), in which segments of circles and narrow bars of colour overlap in varying degrees of brightness and transparency. Like Pevsner and Gabo, Moholy-Nagy tried out a number of different solutions to the problem of representing light and of embodying the dynamic principles of life in art. He did so following an intensive study of Malevich and the Russian Constructivists, prior to his joining the Bauhaus in 1923.

Despite their contact with non-figurative and geometric art, Feininger, Schlemmer and Klee never completely gave up referring to reality. Feininger's landscapes are distinguished by the balanced integration of colour and light in dynamic compositions. Early on, he had concerned himself with the pictorial solutions offered by the Orphic Cubism of Delaunay and with the agitated surfaces of Futurist pictures but, in his urban landscapes and seascapes, he approached more closely the landscape painting of the German Romantics. His inclusion of medieval towers in his townscapes is a reference to these forerunners. In 1911 Feininger became acquainted with the art of Robert Delaunay. Like many artists in Germany, he followed the direction Delaunay had taken with his Parisian townscapes and their colourful Orphic Cubism. From 1929 to 1931 he painted eleven views of Halle in his atmospheric, light-filled style. *Towers over the Town* (1931) belongs to this series of urban landscapes, which arose from his transfiguration of rigorous Cubist formalism.

The ascendancy of architecture propagated at the Bauhaus and within the other Constructivist groups determined not only Feininger's choices of subject, but also those of Schlemmer who, on the basis of his involvement with the Bauhaus stage, concentrated exclusively on the problem of figures in space. The human body, simplified like an idol, became the central element in his pictures. Ideal space and a plastic conception of the human body interact in ever new ways. Rationally organized compositions and mystically inspirited figures led Schlemmer to a balance which aims, not at the rigorousness of a Mondrian, but at the creation of an irrational interweaving in space of horizontals and verticals, of front and back. *Group of Fourteen* (1930) comes from the period just after Schlemmer's time at the Bauhaus, when a soft, painterly modelling of the figures began to replace the metallic colours of previous years.

As a teacher and artist, Paul Klee reacted in a unique way to the challenge presented by the Bauhaus, with which he was connected from 1920 to 1931. During these years he developed his own theory of art and produced an extensive body of graphic work in an endeavour to communicate the basic principles of art in the form of teaching material. His contact with Cubism and Delaunay and his position within the Blaue Reiter circle had brought him to the very centre of the discussions and movements of modern art. By the time he was called to the Bauhaus, Klee had quite deliberately built up the foundations of his oeuvre. The Bauhaus fostered a systematic clarification and an elaboration of his individual universe, which was permeated by a subtle, sometimes scurrilous, sense of poetry. Although Klee concerned himself with the rational analysis of art, he nevertheless took part in the Surrealist exhibition of 1925 in Paris. In its variety, his work reflects the unique multiplicity of his talents, which encompassed music and painting, poetry and theoretical writings. *Fool in a Trance,* of 1929, combines loving skill and a seemingly rational linear architecture to produce free-floating figurative associations. The 'musical' rhythms of colour and line give birth to a creature whose weightless body appears as a fleeting apparition on the very limits of visibility. From the same year, 1929, comes Klee's masterpiece of the time, *Highway and Byways.* Memories of a journey to Egypt in 1928-29 combine with a pictorial construction based on the proportionality of its elements to create an incomparable symbol of the South. On a light-reflecting gesso ground Klee applied gently broken harmonies of blue and yellow, enriched by a lively relief of scratches in the soft plaster ground. Ground and painting merge to form a wonderful unity, a unity which, despite the calculated pictorial architecture, contains the germ of that exceptional freedom which was to characterize the works created in the loneliness of his last years in Switzerland.

While Klee's work went far beyond Constructivism in the narrow sense of the term, other artists were discovering their own form of Constructivist picture by orientating themselves on Dutch and French models or, later, on the French group Abstraction-Création.

Berlin occupied a special position within Constructivist art. It was here that Erich Buchholz had formative artistic experiences after 1921. His *Relief* of that year is a severe combination of the plastic effect of its material with the black and red used to colour it.

From Berlin, connections developed to the circle around Schwitters in Hanover and, through the presence of numerous Russian artists in the city, to East European countries. The lively internationalism of the European art world in the twenties is also personified by the names of Otto Freundlich and František Kupka. Like many a German artist, the latter was captivated by Delaunay's art. His own artistic roots in Symbolism and *Jugendstil* united with impressions of French art to produce work that is best described as 'musical'. *Red and Green* of 1919 still bears witness to this multiplicity of influences, whereas *Musical Box* (1946) shows Kupka's later indebtedness to the cool geometry of French Abstraction-Création.

Another important wanderer in inter-war Europe was Otto Freundlich. Alternating between Germany and Paris as he did, Freundlich belonged to various groups of artists in both France and Germany. His versatile mind, which touched on such subjects as religion, social utopias and the dialectics of rational discourse, was not only reflected in his writings, but also lent his visual work an unusually wide formal range. The abstract conception of his pictures interacts with an Expressionist feeling for the world. In the years 1919-20, which were so important to the Dada movement around Max Ernst, Freundlich also maintained contact with Cologne, where he was attracted to the Social Constructivism of Heinrich Hoerle and Franz Wilhelm Seiwert. These two artists were decisively involved in the birth of the group known as the *Rheinische Progressive* ('Rhineland Prog-ressives'). This association of artists working in a 'constructive' manner left the Dada movement in order to go their own way with themes drawn from society. Seiwert's *Town and Country* of 1932 is an exemplary realization of their aims. Freundlich himself spent his last years in Paris, creating such works as *Green-Red,* which demonstrates his ability to imbue abstract material with a feeling of what he called 'cosmic communism'. In France, this art influenced people like Gaston Chaissac and Serge Poliakoff, but its effects have also been felt in new German art since 1960 – for example, in the early sculptures of Antonius Höckelmann.

European abstract art was uprooted by the far-reaching political upheavals that began in the early thirties: they separated the avant-garde of East and West, and the Fascist threat destroyed all visions of a social utopia.

The next chapter in the history of abstract painting was to be written in the United States, where the New York school of Abstract Expressionism supplanted and developed the art of the Russian avant-garde and of European Surrealism.

81   Paul Klee, *Highway and Byways*, 1929, 83 × 67 cm

82   Paul Klee
Fool in a Trance, 1929, 50.5 × 35.5 cm

83   Lyonel Feininger
Bridge III, 1917, 80.5 × 100 cm

84   Lyonel Feininger, *Towers over the Town (Halle)*, 1931, 88.3 × 124 cm

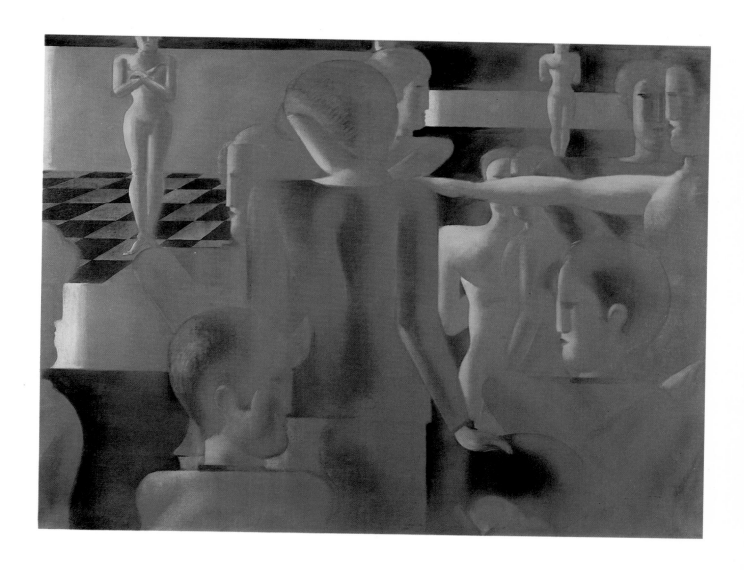

85   Oskar Schlemmer, *Group of Fourteen in Imaginary Architecture*, 1930, 91.5 × 120.5 cm

86   František Kupka, *Red and Green,* 1913, 46 × 38 cm

87   František Kupka, *Musical Box*, 1946, 51.4 × 50 cm

88   László Moholy-Nagy
On a White Ground, 1923, 101 × 80.5 cm

89   Piet Mondrian
Tableau I, 1921, 96.5 × 60.5 cm

90   Otto Freundlich,
Rise, 1929, Height 200 cm

91   Otto Freundlich
Green-Red, 1939, 65 × 54.4 cm

92   Heinrich Hoerle, *Masks,* 1929, 68.5 × 95.5 cm

93   Franz-Wilhelm Seiwert, *Town and Country,* 1932, 70.6 × 80.7 cm

5

Max Ernst, Dada and Surrealism

The Dada movement first made its appearance in Zurich during the First World War. In this major city of neutral Switzerland, intellectuals, artist, poets and writers had congregated in their flight from the self-destructive forces that had been unleashed in the rest of Europe. Dada arose out of a feeling of collapse resulting from historical upheavals which seemed to signify the end of the bourgeois era. When Hugo Ball founded the literary night-club Cabaret Voltaire in 1916, the main impulses of the movement came from writers. Initially, the visual arts did not react with a comparably acute awareness of the crisis. A number of events served to bring them on a level with literary achievements: Duchamp's invention of the 'ready-made', the arrival of Francis Picabia in Zurich from New York in 1917, exhibitions of works by Max Ernst, Johannes Baargeld and Hans Arp in Cologne in 1919-20, and the presentation of Kurt Schwitters 'Merz' works in 1919.

The use of banal, everyday objects as works of art, and the irrational, incongruous combination of fragments of reality and dreams in collages, were the artistic means used by the Dadaists to combat the decorative aestheticism of Cubism.

Although the name 'Dada' was first used in Zurich, Marcel Duchamp, Man Ray and Francis Picabia had already been working in a Dadaistic mode in New York. As early as 1913, Duchamp produced his first ready-made: a bicycle mounted on a kitchen stool. In turning his back on painting in this way, he created a radical alternative to it which has occupied artists ever since.

The New York artists had been producing Dada without realizing it. It was Picabia's journey to Europe in 1917 which led to direct contact with the movement itself. Duchamp's *Bicycle* had still been based on the studies of motion in Cubo-Futurist painting, since not only could the bicycle still be set in motion, but this very motion was the essence of the work. The following objects, like the *Bottle Drier* and *Urinal*, Duchamp selected from the world of everyday things without changing them in any way. The addition of the artist's signature allowed them to cross the threshold into 'art'.

Man Ray, who had been working with Duchamp since 1916, exerted considerable influence by virtue of his various experiments, which included work with film and photography. He was also responsible for some ready-mades. In 1919, for example, he hung a damaged lamp-shade from the ceiling of his New York studio in such a way as to create a spiral form. He returned frequently to this motif, also using it in pictures – *Retour à la Raison,* for instance.

Picabia occupied an important place in the Dada movement both in New York and Zurich. As painted ready-mades, so to speak, his adaptations of machines, technical drawings and technological objects for pictorial purposes attacked prevailing concepts of style. He negated, as did Duchamp, that expectation of 'beautiful' pictures which played a rudimentary, but nonetheless significant, part in Cubism. Around 1922 the work of both the European and New York Dadaists changed; they were, in fact, taking the first steps towards Surrealism. Picabia's *The Spanish Night* comes from this transitional phase. One of his first figurative pictures, it yet retains links with the mechanistic Dadaist works in its sharp separation of colours and in its inclusion of targets and writing. If Picabia's subsequent figurative pictures, as exemplified by *The Bride* (1929), were not regarded very highly, then that was due to the gap between his stylistic and artistic standpoint and that of the Surrealist group in Paris which, from 1922 onwards, attracted ever more artists to its cause. The Surrealists defined the subconscious as the new source of art, propagating the idea with exceptional vehemence. The change from Dada to Surrealism, with its basis in a systematic theory, was accomplished under the leadership of the poet André Breton.

Between 1919 and 1922 Max Ernst, who came from Brühl, near Cologne, had been in the front line of the fascinating development from the anarchy of Dada to the literary ideas of Surrealism. From his artistic beginnings within the wider circle of the Rhineland Expressionists, he had addressed himself to the formal problems raised by the new French art. The radiant colours and lyricism of Delaunay's Cubism lie behind the urban landscape *Laon,* which Ernst painted in 1916 while a soldier in France. Only after the end of the war was he able to continue his systematic search for an individual path of his own. Decisive steps on this road were taken in 1919 with his Dadaistic collages. He discovered relief printing and 'frottage' (tracings produced by rubbing) as acceptable artistic means of giving concrete form to his restless optical powers of association. During the short Dada period he did so by means of arresting confrontations between the various parts of a picture. However, in 1921-22, when Ernst turned to painting as the chief medium for realizing his pictorial ideas, the provocative fortuity of the collages developed into an imagery with roots in philosophy and in Freud's psychology. Although seemingly devoid of logic, this imagery in fact obeys the deep-seated laws of the human psyche.

Ernst's monumental *Rendezvous of Friends,* which he began after his arrival in Paris in August 1922, is one of the most important visual manifestos of Surrealism, documenting the intimate relationship between the worlds of poetry, philosophy and painting which characterized the movement. Neatly numbered and identified on the scrolls at the sides of the picture, the leading Surrealists appear here accompanied by the figures of Raphael and Dostoevsky from the past. The mysterious gestures and allusions, the bizarre setting on a mountain peak and the backdrop of portentous constellations of stars add up to a most imposing image. The composition refers to Raphael's *Disputà* and Leonardo's *Last Supper,* but an intangible irony arising from the obscure gestures and the puppet-like woodenness of the figures guards against the merest suspicion of historicism. The artist's father, who was an amateur painter, had copied the *Disputà,* and this must have made such a deep impression on Ernst that the memory of it lived on even in a surrealistically fragmented context. On the one hand, Ernst's interest in 'classical' art allowed him to return to a pre-Cubist form of painting while, on the other, his ironically detached, yet poetic, allusions to that art negated the pathos of classical aesthetics.

In 1926 Max Ernst once more drew upon a classical iconographic type in *The Virgin Beating the Christ Child in Front of Three Witnesses: André Breton, Paul Eluard and the Painter.* Art historians are familiar with the theme under the title 'Venus Chastising Cupid'. The Christian title chosen by Ernst hints at a settling of accounts with his strict Catholic upbringing, but, above all, points to the sexual entanglements and traumatic experiences which, in classical treatments of the subject, remain hidden behind a beautiful exterior. The style of the picture is governed by the contrast between the rounded bodies and the flatly painted architecture, with the witnesses glimpsed through a window in it. The painting appears rather abruptly among Ernst's works in 1926, being more closely related to such earlier pictures as *Rendezvous of Friends* than to the products of the frottage technique which he was exploring so extensively at the time. In these frottages Surrealist fantasy lets itself be swept into visions of nature which were taken up again in a work like *Water-plants* of 1929. This uses oil colour applied with the palette-knife to achieve the effects previously produced by frottage in the *Histoire naturelle* of 1925. The harmony between Surrealist fantasy as expressed in Ernst's individual *écriture automatique* and expanded painting techniques gave rise to a poetic richness which was, in fact, the chief goal of his basically romantic painting.

A chance encounter with reproductions of works by Giorgio de Chirico in a Munich bookshop in 1919 had proved one of the decisive experiences on Max Ernst's path to Surrealism. The series of etchings *Fiat modes, pereat ars* (1919) lies completely under the spell of de Chirico, whose work from 1911 onwards had embodied an individual and wilful method foreshadowing that of Surrealism. The Italian brought together objects originating in various areas of the mind and placed them in illogical and non-literary contexts: only the sense of an underlying affinity between the elements lent the pictures a certain unity. Furthermore, the compositions were carried out in a style which may be understood both as a parody of Renaissance perspective painting and, perhaps, as a longing for its return. De Chirico seemed to break with all the advances made by Modernism and its Parisian manifestations. Nevertheless, his style exuded such fascination that, despite being considerably different from Surrealism, it contributed to the latter's development. De Chirico was especially influential in that branch of Surrealism which sought to maintain contact with realistic pictorial imagery as a means of making dreams visible. Besides Dali and Ernst, the Belgians Magritte and Delvaux, and the Frenchman Yves Tanguy, belonged to this 'Flemish' Surrealism. The other branch of the movement, orientated more towards drawing, was interested in spontaneous inspiration. Miró, Masson and Klee may be reckoned among its exponents.

Miró's *Love,* of 1926, is confined entirely to the basic constituents of painting: a harmony of blue tones on unprimed canvas acquires a telling radiance by the addition of only a few suggestions of lines, letters and figures. The pictures of Dali, Magritte, Delvaux and Tanguy, on the other hand, are prominent examples of the realistic, almost photographic style of Surrealist painting. The possibilities of this style range from Magritte's cooly calculated analogies – for example, *La présence d'esprit* (1960), in which man, fish and bird are combined like hieroglyphs – to huge works of great complexity, such as Salvador Dali's *Perpignan Station* of 1965. In a breathtaking vision of perspective spaces, horizons and brilliantly painted shifts in degrees of reality, he conjures up his world of images in a pictorial credo based on a personal, highly erotic interpretation of the famous picture *Angelus* by François Millet. The peasant and his wife, the figures on the extreme right and left of the painting, and the wheelbarrow and sacks are all derived from Millet's work. The crucified Christ appears in schematic form in the centre, a cross-shaped shaft of light gliding across his face. The falling (or rising) figure of the artist is seen at the brightest point of this light-beam. Only the railway carriage points to the station of the title. Dali often passed through Perpignan station and, owing to a mysterious connection with the only existing sketch by Sigmund Freud, he viewed it as symbol of artistic inspiration.

The realistic variant of Surrealism continued to be immensely influential after its appearance in the second half of the twenties. The Dada movement had burnt itself out in only a few years, but some of its protagonists persevered in implementing the principle of poetry produced by the juxtaposition of apparently incongruous elements. Kurt Schwitters must rank as the one Dada artist who remained genuinely and consistently true to its ideas all his life. *The Great Ich Picture (Merz Picture 9b)* of 1919 belongs among the major works of his earlier period, in which he created Cubo-Futurist images out of pieces of paper, fragments of letters of the alphabet, advertisements and tickets. At this time Schwitters sought to achieve formal correlations between the chromatic and formal values of the collage elements and the pictorial structure itself. Later, in such works as *Glass Flower* of 1940, the 'found objects' were allowed greater independence and thus addressed the beholder more directly. Those American and European artists of the fifties who used Dada's strategy in attempting to put an end to the dominance of abstract art in the post-war period admired these late works by Schwitters, seeing in them a justification of the path they had taken.

The dreamily intricate work of the American Joseph Cornell also contributed to the revival of interest in collage. He mounted poetic momentos of great nineteenth-century hotels in small boxes. On this miniature scale he conjured up a large imaginary space, on the boundaries of which there lies, for example, the *Ocean Hotel* in Ostend.

94   Max Ernst, *Laon*, 1916, 65.6 × 100.5 cm

1 René Crevel
2 Philippe Soupault
3 Arp
4 Max Ernst
5 Max Morise
6 Fédor Dostoïewski
7 Raffaele Sanzio
8 Théodore Fraenkel
9 Paul Eluard
10 Jean Paulhan

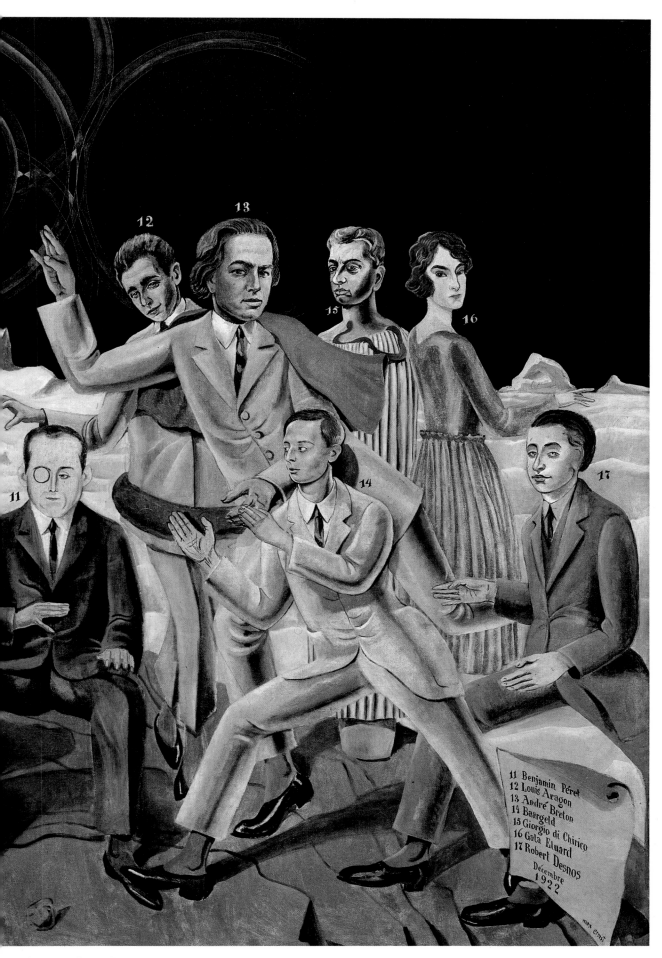

95   Max Ernst, *The Rendezvous of Friends*, 1923, 130 × 195 cm

96   Max Ernst, *Birth of Comedy*, 1947, 53 × 40 cm

97   Max Ernst, *The Virgin Beating the Christ Child in Front of Three Witnesses:*
André Breton, Paul Eluard and the Painter, 1926, 196 × 130 cm

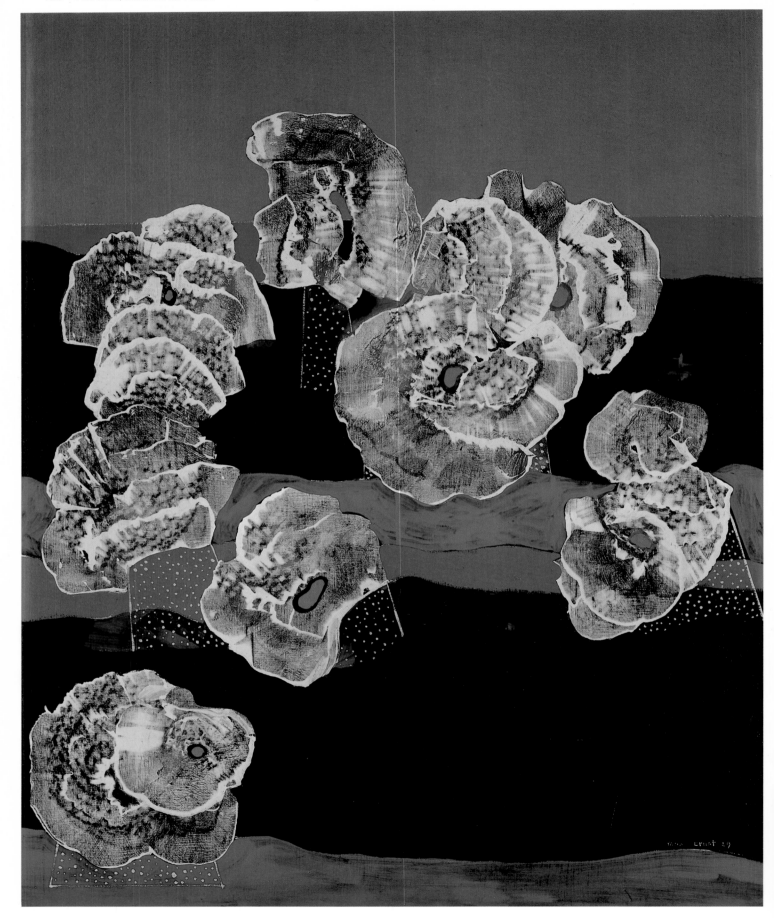

98　Max Ernst, *Water-plants*, 1929, 100 × 80 cm

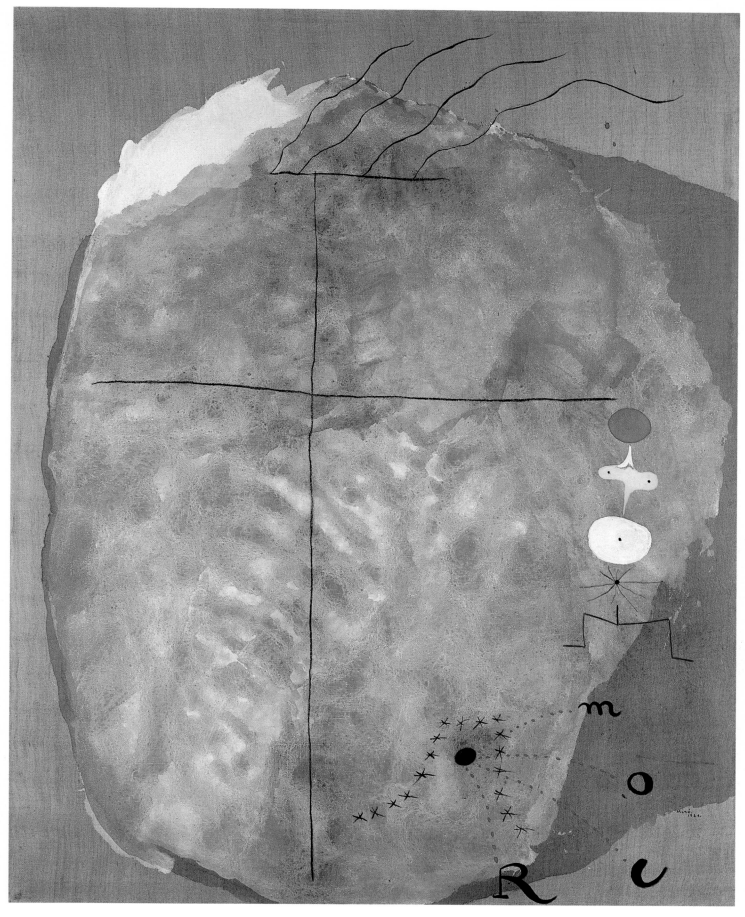

99   Joan Miró, *Love*, 1926, 146 × 114 cm

100 Kurt Schwitters, *The Great Ich Picture*
(Merz Picture 9b), 1919, 96.8 × 70 cm

101   Kurt Schwitters
Glass Flower, 1940, 77.5 × 67.5 × 25.5 cm

102   Marcel Duchamp, *The Portable Museum*
1964, 41 x 37.8 x 10.5 cm

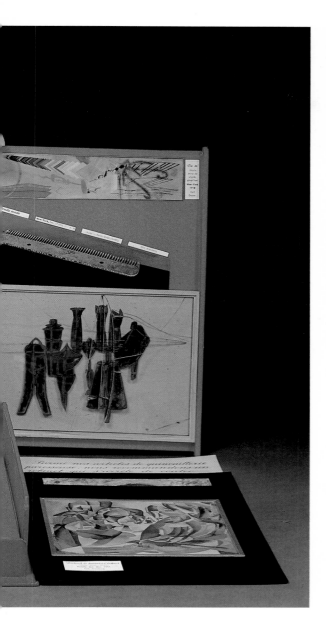

103   Marcel Duchamp
Bicycle, 1913/1964, Height 126.5 cm

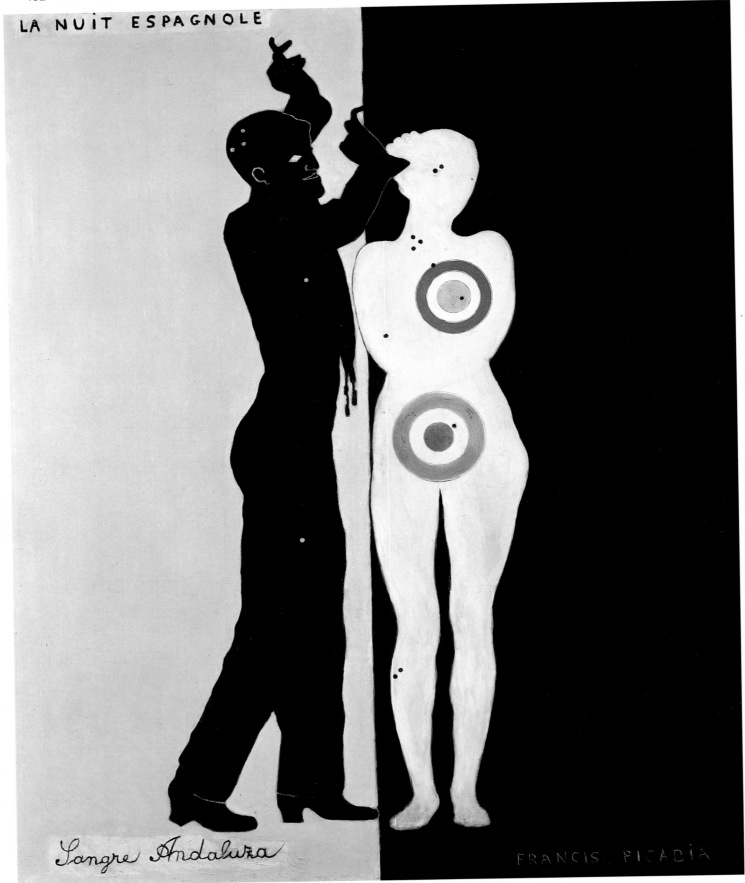

104   Francis Picabia, *The Spanish Night*, 1922, 200 × 161 cm

LA MARIÉE

Francis Picabia

105   Francis Picabia, *The Bride*, c. 1929, 121.5 × 96.5 cm

106   Giorgio de Chirico, *Roman Comedy*, 1926, 146.5 x 114.5 cm

107   Alberto Savinio, *Ulysses and Polyphemus*, 1929, 65 × 81 cm

108   René Magritte, *La présence d'esprit*, 1960, 116 x 89 cm

109   Paul Delvaux, *The Forest Nymphs,* 1966, 149.5 × 237.5 cm

110   Hans Arp, *Nadir Relief*
1959, 152.5 × 130.5 cm

111   Hans Arp
Female Torso, 1953 (1930), Height 88 cm

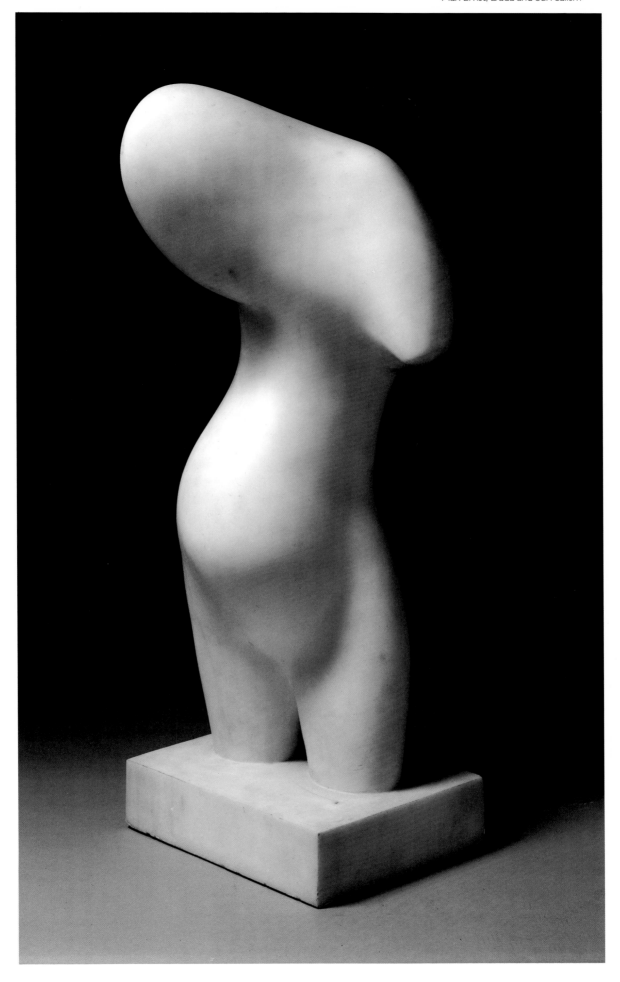

112   Alberto Giacometti
The Nose, 1947, 38 × 7.5 × 66 cm

113   Alberto Giacometti
Square, 1950, 56.2 × 56 × 42.5 cm

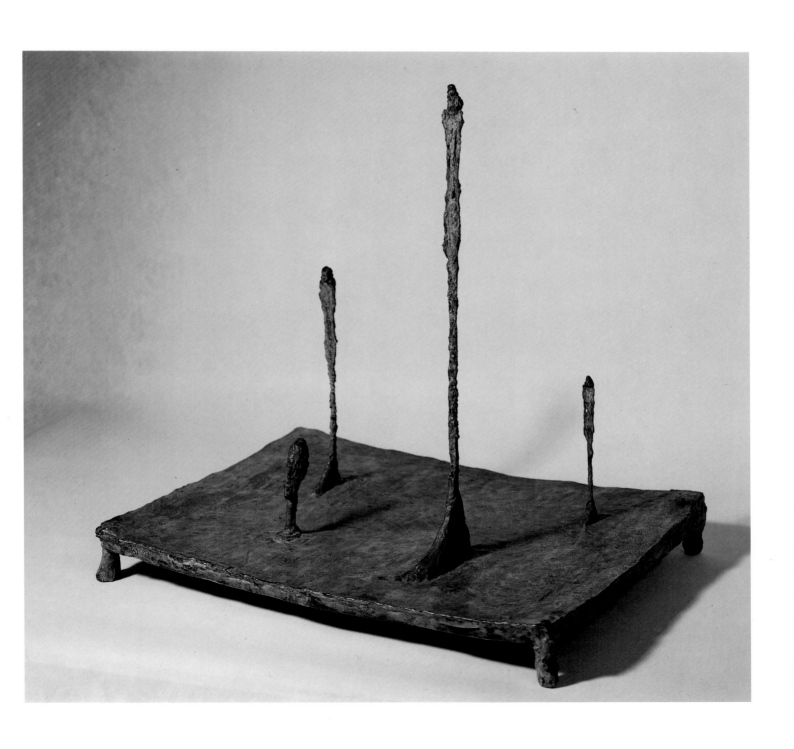

114   Salvador Dali, *Perpignan Station*
1965, 295 × 406 cm

115   Joseph Cornell, *Ocean Hotel,* 1959/60, 21.5 × 36 × 10.2 cm

6

Abstract Art in America

During the forties and fifties, a group of New York artists of quite different temperaments and from various backgrounds developed a new, specifically American conception of what constitutes an 'image'. In Europe, they became known as the New York School. Art critics found themselves faced with a novel form of abstraction which rejected on principle the notion that art must spring from individual personality or from society. As these artists saw it, art should realize only itself, without attempting to interfere with reality. Their new style – also called Abstract Expressionism or Action Painting – broke completely with the social subject matter that had dominated American painting in the thirties. They were guided by approaches and conclusions drawn from Cubism, Fauvism, Surrealism and Russian revolutionary art. Parallel to the Existentialist painting developed during the Second World War in Europe by Picasso, Fautrier, Wols and Dubuffet, there appeared a new style of painting in New York which was similarly inspired by Existentialist attitudes to society. Not only totally isolated from, but also virtually ignored by, American society at large, and in the midst of a world threatening to destroy itself through war, a radical art of self-expression came into being which, with its explosive power, invalidated all the existing rules of a hitherto rather provincial American art. Left very much to themselves, the artists of the new school drew great artistic and moral freedom from their isolation.

The formal means and discoveries of the New York School derived from the most heterogeneous sources and developed into a highly complex phenomenon as a result of the contrary temperaments involved. Pollock's uncompromising extension of European 'psychic automatism' in his 'dripping pictures' represents one extreme of this phenomenon. The opposite pole is exemplified by the meditative use of colour, influenced by Jewish mysticism, that can be found in the work of Newman and Rothko. De Kooning, Gorky, Franz Kline and Motherwell are all closer to Pollock, whereas Ad Reinhardt and Clifford Still both show points of contact with meditative abstraction.

The path to an independent American abstraction began with the activities of two German artists in the United States during the thirties. Hans Hofmann founded his art school in New York in 1934, and Josef Albers had been a teacher at the Black Mountain College in North Carolina since 1933. In his style, Hofmann combined the planar conception of Cubism with a radiant use of colour inspired by Fauvism. Albers had arrived at a comprehensive theory of the interrelation between colour, plane, proportion and perception while teaching at the Bauhaus. In the midst of realistic American art of the thirties, these two Germans laid the foundations of a new awareness of the possibilities inherent in abstraction. As mentors of the new generation of artists, both teachers emphasized the interaction between a creative act and the artist's position as the first to apprehend that act. In other words, painting resulted from the give and take between artist and work. Later, in the sixties, this idea was extended to include the participation of the beholder in apprehending a work, but the first steps towards supplanting traditional painting on canvas or other supports were taken in early post-war New York. The picture no longer opened an imaginary window onto something outside the wall of the room in which it was located but, rather, became the wall itself, to be experienced by a viewer moving about in the room in front of the picture. Surface texture acquires a new and increased significance as a result of this re-evaluation. Whether treated in monochrome, shaped by the sweeping movements of dripping or fashioned by impetuous gestures, the texture of the paint is what communicates the essential message to the beholder. This constitutes the new quality of these works.

It was Jackson Pollock who departed most radically from his European Modernist forerunners. Even though the dripping technique had been employed sporadically before, Pollock was the first to sense and utilize its full formative potential in the creation of pictures. Some Abstract Expressionists approached their work on the basis of Surrealism's *écriture automatique,* although this brought with it the danger of founding expression in literary associations. A few of these artists never managed to go beyond giving form to signals from the sub-conscious and thus did not help to extend the concept 'picture'. Pollock, on the other hand, had expunged the last traces of iconography from his pictures in 1947, so that they became densely textured objects of line and colour. He wished to force the antithetical psychic impulses governing human activity and the world to come together again in his paintings. This Romanticism lent his work an aura and an existential dimension which made him the central figure of his generation.

Willem de Kooning, who came to New York from Rotterdam, drew on the faceted planar structures of Cubism and, like Pollock, developed them in the direction of standardization. Whereas Cubism fragmented reality in order to accomodate it to the picture plane, Pollock and de Kooning took the faceted picture plane itself, with its myriad focal points, as their point of departure, without subjecting it to a limiting comparison with reality. Consequently, the picture appeared as an excerpt from a continuum, an excerpt determined in each case by the artist in order to give a work its particular character. Not only Pollock's numbered pictures and de Kooning's series, but also Mother-well's more than one hundred *Elegies to the Spanish Republic* and Newman's or Rothko's oeuvre can be interpreted in these terms.

At first glance, it seems paradoxical that painting intended to give unrestrained expression to the emotional and human potential of its creators should result in completely detached, purified form. Here was an abstract realism, made up of surface and colour, which had its expressive origins in *écriture automatique*. This can be seen clearly in the *Elegies* by Motherwell, whose untiring endeavour was to integrate suggestive bent or rounded forms into the mainly black and white stripes of his picture planes. The interaction of randomly produced forms with the pattern of vertical stripes had to be balanced anew in each work. De Kooning never imposed such strict rules on the aggressive gestures of his painting. He allowed the traces left by his brushstrokes to play a decisive part in the final effect, as did Franz Kline, who, again like Motherwell, deliberately developed his pictures out of the contrast between black and white.

The other direction taken by the New York School, that of geometric abstraction, attempted to give new life to the meditative qualities of colour. It was rooted, not in the Surrealist notion of an iconography created 'automatically', but in a belief in the aura and power of colour. Newman's *Midnight Blue* does not constitute an abstract depiction of a particular motif or subject, since no such references are included. The picture plane, and the ordering and balancing of colours produced by the artist's intuition, determine the appearance of the work, which seeks to evoke experiences beyond reality.

Rothko shares with Newman an absolute refusal to equate painting with the imitation of nature. In the end, he tolerated only an immaterial confrontation between a few colours, these becoming increasingly dark towards the close of his career. With the aid of its carefully arranged colours, the painting *Earth and Green,* characterized by a simple layering of areas of colour, produces the impression of spaces of great emotional tension which appeal to religious feelings. In the work of both Newman and Rothko, the heritage of Jewish mysticism makes itself felt in a radiance of colour which was developed over a period of many years within a highly disciplined formal framework.

The generation of abstract artists that took the stage around 1960 had divested itself of the expressive elements apparent in the works of its predecessors. Frank Stella set a radical example with his *Black Pictures* of 1958-59, which go beyond even Ad Reinhardt's recourse to the 'black picture' as the ultimate in painting. In Reinhardt's work, black still contains traces of colour, so that rather than documenting the demise of the picture, they seem to capture a moment shortly before its final disappearance. By contrast, Stella treats black as real in itself, without investing it with the mystery of colour or the emotion of form. The picture becomes identical with the support, which determines its format. In *Bonin Night Heron no. 1,* produced twenty years after the *Black Pictures,* Stella goes so far as to give the individual forms of the picture objective reality by letting their cut-out shapes protrude and recede in order to create a relief.

Like Stella, Morris Louis reached the stage where the form of the picture and the picture support became an inextricable unity. Although his creative life was relatively short, Louis, together with Kenneth Noland, achieved a terse, extremely attractive form of abstraction in a startling and seemingly simply way. On the basis of Helen Frankenthaler's method of soaking unprimed canvases in pigment, Louis arrived at his technique of allowing abstract motifs to emerge from the natural run of the paint on the canvas. A more complete integration of paint and support can hardly be imagined. *Pillar of Dawn* (1961) employs this method to produce an image of suggestive power: the rivulets of resonant colour were turned upside down after they had run their course.

Having consolidated itself around 1950 into the first specifically American style of Abstract Expressionism, art in New York split into three quite different directions in the period after 1960. Abstraction continued its development in the creation of terse ciphers. From the mid-fifties onwards, a renewed interest in Dada took as its point of departure not only European achievements, but also the activities of Duchamp and Picabia in New York around 1912. These two approaches were supplemented from about the middle of the sixties by the emergence of Minimal Art, which had been heralded by such works as Frank Stella's *Black Pictures*.

Sol LeWitt, Donald Judd and Walter de Maria contributed decisively to the creation of minimalist sculpture. Richard Serra links his reduction of sculpture to the meaning inherent in its materials to Minimal Art. In the past two decades, this form of art has had an immeasurable influence through its radical integration of ideas and their manifestations in space. The art of the eighties has been determined to a large extent by Minimal Art and Conceptual Art. The latent spirituality, the symbolism and the contemplative openness of works like Walter de Maria's *Pentagon* or Sol LeWitt's *3 Part Set* (1968) led, strangely enough, to conclusions which permitted a return to figurative art.

Richard Serra's *Moe,* a breathtaking balancing act of massive iron plates, seems to break in upon this lively give-and-take of artistic approaches like a primeval event, transforming material into awesome modern monuments. The roughness and apparent clumsiness of such sculptures may provoke fear and a defensive attitude in the beholder, but these are overcome in the end by the plastic richness of the volumes, by the variety of the space created and by the totally matter-of-fact presence of the materials, which take on an almost mythical aura. The result is a most extreme experience of sculpture's potential when it excludes external themes or aesthetic effects. American abstract art has here reached a point so far removed from the visible world, with not even the most indirect allusions to it, that the dominance of the material – paint, canvas or metal – itself seems to represent a kind of crass realism.

116   Willem de Kooning, *Untitled VI*, 1984, 203 × 178 cm

117   Barnett Newman, *Midnight Blue,* 1970, 193 x 239 cm

118 Mark Rothko, *Earth and Green*, 1955, 231.5 × 187 cm

119   Jackson Pollock,
Unformed Figure, 1953, 132 × 195.2 cm

120   Frank Stella
Seven Steps, 1959, 216 × 156.5 cm

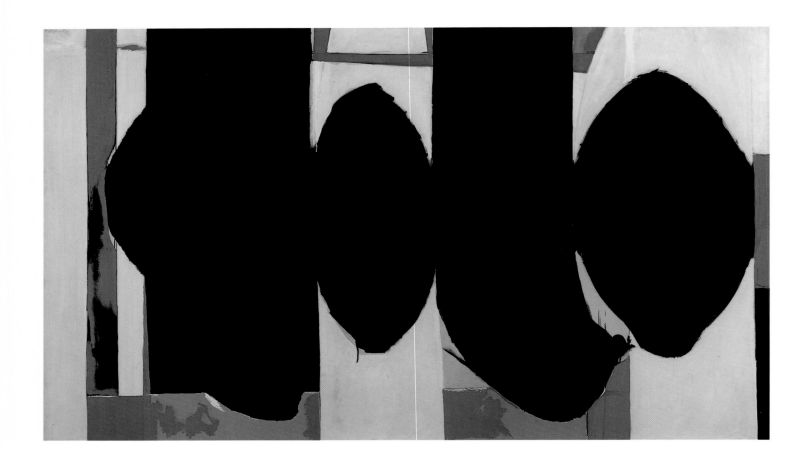

121   Robert Motherwell
Elegy to the Spanish Republic, 1953/54, 209 x 351 cm

122   Morris Louis
Pillar of Dawn, 1961, 220 x 122 cm

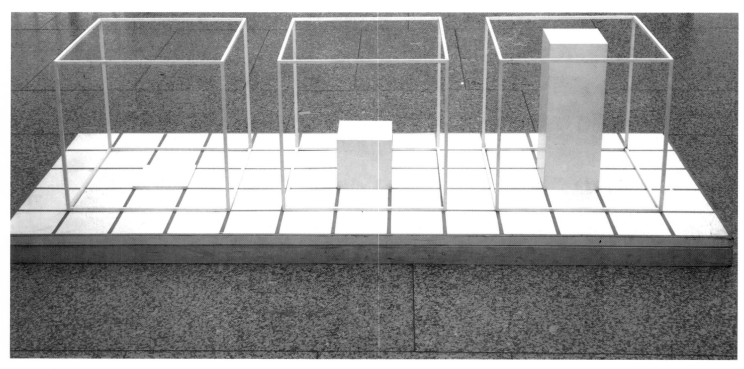

123   Donald Judd, *Untitled*
(Eight Modular Unit), 1966-68, 120 × 313 × 318 cm

124   Sol LeWitt
3 Part Set, 1968, 80 × 208 × 50 cm

125   Richard Serra
Moe, 1971, 244 × 610 × 366 cm

126   Frank Stella, *Bonin Night Heron no. 1*, 1976, 275 × 350 × 65 cm

7

Europe became acquainted with new American painting directly after the end of the Second World War through, for example, the exhibition of the Peggy Guggenheim Collection and various gallery shows in France and Italy. The first such exhibition in Berlin took place in 1951, while in 1958-59 the now legendary show 'The New American Painting' toured the cities of Europe, including Berlin. It was in this way that Pollock's work became known in Europe. Although developments in the direction of the new American style had already been underway in Europe during the war, European abstract art did of course react to this fresh impulse. Two emigrant German artists, Hans Hartung and Wols, had made very distinguished contributions to upholding the tradition of European abstract art at a time when those countries with Fascist governments contented themselves with the heroic posturings of a shallow classicism. Both artists had fled to Paris in the 1930s – Hartung somewhat earlier than Wols – and it was there that each arrived at a personal pictorial language.

Hartung reached his individual style via an Expressionist early phase which, although figurative, included a contemplative abstract component. In 1922 he painted his first abstract works, in which patches of colour and large script-like signs united to form gently vibrant compositions. As in the beginnings of American Abstract Expressionism around 1940, the influence of Kandinsky's early work is unmistakable in these pictures. Hartung retained their lyrical, romantic tone even when his compositions became increasingly simple and evocative of pent-up energies. A work such as *T 56-21* (1956) bears witness to a high level of artistry in the free placing of graphic elements to fill the picture with a delicate equilibrium. Only to a certain extent does Hartung allow himself to be drawn into the chaos of abstract gestures governing the picture space. By taming these potentially disruptive abstract energies, he succeeded in creating a relaxed, effortless pictorial architecture that left behind both the cool calculation of Bauhaus abstraction and the symbolic approach inherited from Kandinsky's Munich period.

Besides being a writer and musician, Wols (i. e. Wolfgang Schulze) worked as a photographer and an art teacher before turning to painting in about 1939. After an initial Surrealist phase, his work took on a style which may be recognized as an early form of Art informel. His art expresses itself in the injured, beaten surface of a picture. *The Blue Phantom* (1951) appears like a wound in the body of the painting – symbol of the existential isolation of this painter, who loved Rimbaud and saw himself as heir to those *peintres maudits* who, since the Romantic era, had been so much a part of the concept of the rejected and despised artist.

These two German artists became the centre of a movement which, under the name École de Paris, was to dominate the aesthetics of post-war European art for a long time. Designations such as Tachisme (French *tache* = stain, blot), Art informel and Un art autre were applied to this movement which, attracting numerous artists, became increasingly diffuse in character. Hartung was regarded as the instigator of Tachisme, Wols as the father of Art informel. One particularly individual style of signs was created by Pierre Soulages who, like Hartung, placed graphic elements on a uniform ground reminiscent of Franz Kline in its concentrated power. The Canadian Jean-Pierre Riopelle, in Paris from 1947, combined the 'all-over' evenness of Pollock's picture surfaces with the physical qualities of glowing colours applied directly to the canvas before being worked on with the palette-knife. As a final element, the artist strung fine threads of colour over the glistening relief. In one series of paintings, Riopelle expressly referred to Monet's *Nymphéas,* while the colourfulness of his works and the plastic intensity of their surfaces recall the abstract compositions of Otto Freundlich.

Isolated like Wols, Nicolas de Staël was also active in Paris at this time. As with many important painters who worked there during the first half of the century – for example, Kandinsky, Chagall, Sonia Delaunay and Ossip Zadkine – de Staël came from Russia and, like Serge Poliakoff, made an individual contribution to post-war painting in the French capital. He used flat areas of colour, sometimes applied in heavy impasto, in his confrontation of the visible world – especially in his last years, after he had brought together bright colours as if in a mosaic. The still life *L'Étagère,* from the last year of de Staël's life, exemplifies this concise style, although it lacks the bright colours. It presents the motif reduced to the the barest essentials and, despite its restrained aura, remains allied to the French spirit of Braque's still lifes.

At the end of the Second World War, German art found itself in a seemingly hopeless situation. For almost ten years the Hitler regime had divided art into the 'national' *(völkisch)* and the 'degenerate'. The best painters and sculptors had left Germany, and those who did not were either forbidden to work, went underground or resigned in the face of the system's coercive power.

The fresh start after the collapse of the Third Reich belongs among both the most tragic and the most surprising episodes in the history of German art. Re-entry into the international mainstream was accomplished at an astonishingly early date and marked by a variety of approaches. The majority of artists employed the abstract method, often passing through an initial phase of Surrealism in a moderate form. It was only in the course of the fifties that art in the two German states took on the character of a doctrine, so that realism and abstraction eventually hardened into ideological positions in east and west respectively. However, the finest artists were not content to accept such orthodoxies, but rather reflected on their own situation following the catastrophe which had shattered their country. Thus, Wilhelm Nay, while still on military service in France, took important steps towards overcoming the planar Expressionism he had developed out of Kirchner's late works. Immediately after the war, paintings on mythical subjects pointed the way towards a pristine splendour of colour which, richly patterned, lent his pictures an extra dimension. *Jacob's Ladder,* dating from 1946, fuses figurative and abstract elements into a whole characterized by a texture which seems to foreshadow his later 'disc pictures'.

Nay's development can be traced through a few well-defined phases, all of which enlarge upon the artistic foundations he had laid in 1945-46. Not until the last years of his life did an apparent break occur in the logical, natural unfolding of his oeuvre. His works of 1964-65, namely, announce a final phase which is marked by a new ordering of the picture plane. In *Check,* for example, its simple arrangement gains shape from a dark ornament which seems to embody in concentrated form all the underlying characteristics of his previous pictures. Nay has a mastery of colour at his disposal which permits comparison with the magical palette of American Abstract Expressionism, although the chromatic contrasts are both more intense and more discordant in his work.

Bernhard Schultze, a second important representative of the post-war generation of artists in Germany, started out from Surrealism, which he saw in an individual way as belonging to the Baroque tradition. Morbid colours combine with a graphic filigree to create fantastic worlds on the edge of the organic. In the fifties, Schultze gave these worlds three-dimensional substance, a title like *Rubyrr* itself evoking the awkwardness of an unusual interaction of figure and space. The broken surface 'landscape' of the picture seems to be enmeshed in a tangle of roots and gives expression to a concern with the physical make-up of the painted surface which had been shared by Klee as much as by Baumeister, Dubuffet or Fautrier. The manner in which Schultze expanded painting in the direction relief constituted a highly original solution to the problem.

127   Hans Hartung, *T 56-21*, 1956, 180 × 114 cm

128   Pierre Soulages, *Painting,* 1964, 202 × 143 cm

129   Jean-Paul Riopelle, *Robe of Stars*, 1952, 200 x 150 cm

130   Ernst Wilhelm Nay, *Jacob's Ladder*, 1964, 96 × 81 cm

131 Ernst Wilhelm Nay, *Check*, 1965, 200 × 162 cm

132   Willi Baumeister, *Standing Figure with Blue Field*, 1933, 82 × 65.5 cm

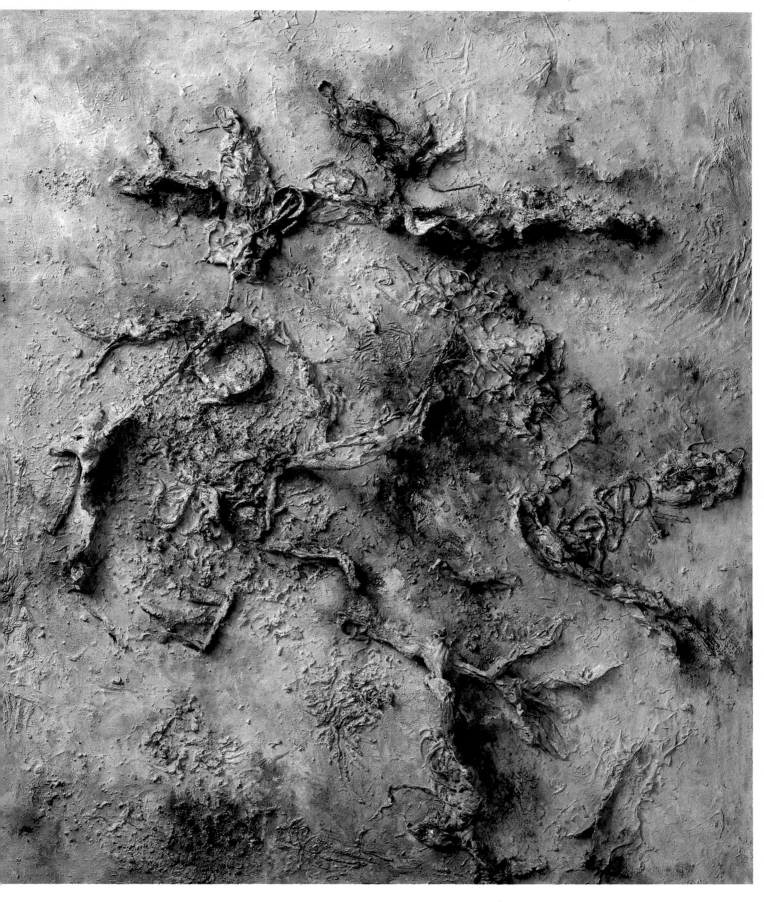

33   Bernard Schultze, *Rubyrr*, 1957/58, 120 × 120 cm

134   Wols, *The Blue Phantom,* 1951, 73 × 60 cm

8

American and English Art of the Sixties

The painting of the New York School not only gave American art a national style, but also earned it an international reputation comparable to that achieved by American literature a generation before. The young artists who, after 1955, set about building on this achievement at first appeared to be rebelling against their abstract forerunners. However, with the benefit of hindsight, the younger generation – and especially Jasper Johns and Robert Rauschenberg – can be seen to have had much in common with the previous one. *Large White Numbers,* a picture Johns painted in 1958, is related in its treatment of surface to Pollock's *Shimmering Substance* of 1946, despite the technique of wax painting and the new, simple subject matter. Similarly, the impulsive use of paint in Rauschenberg's early material pictures recalls the pictorial language of abstract art. Nevertheless, the influence of new ideas from previously untapped sources is unmistakable. *Flag on Orange Field* by Johns or *Odalisque* by Rauschenberg reflect the complex situation towards the end of the fifties, when the general stylistic development was very much in a state of flux. The creation of a new style depended on overcoming the kind of expressivity that had governed the work of Pollock or de Kooning. Apart from a re-evaluation of earlier American realism, it was the intellectual approach of Marcel Duchamp which, as transmitted by John Cage, became a particularly fruitful stimulus for the new aesthetics. The flag picture by Johns combines the turbulent impasto of Abstract Expressionism with a realistically painted flag – a combination of two apparently incompatible elements which poses in a most acute form the question as to what constitutes illusion or reality, surface or object. The philosophical mistrust of painting's illustrative capacities was part of Duchamp's legacy, while the insistence on the picture as a fact in itself had its roots in the strong American tradition of realism. The unusual technique of wax painting, which Johns rediscovered, contributed its share to giving the pictures the character of self-contained concrete entities.

Johns pointed up the problem of realism even more in his sculptures than in his paintings – for example, in *Painted Bronze* of 1960. Transformed into beer cans by the painting, the two cylindrical forms on a plinth emphasize the integrity of the work of art as a concrete object: how can beer cans be art? On the other hand, this provocative effect has become dissipated with time, for today the cans belong, like Picasso's *Absinthe Glass,* among the classic achievements of modern sculpture. Johns's works cannot be judged in 'either/or' terms; they occupy the more ambiguos realm of 'not only… but also'. Thus, the seemingly simple cans are at one and the same time a monument to, and a banal left-over from drinking, are both 'proper' bronze sculpture (as the title, of course, emphasizes) and masterly illusions as a result of the *trompe l'œil* painting. The work is not an 'object sculpture', since its materials were not already manufactured; rather, it is an object created, as it were, artificially. The large works, such as *Edingsville* of 1965 and the four-part *Untitled* of 1972, also bear witness to such intricate matters of perception and feeling. In the latter work, it is the artist's will which relates the optical structures in the four sections to each other, there being no obvious connection between them and no shared meaning in the traditional sense. Starting out from the diagonal shading of the left-hand section, the arrangement of which was inspired by a car ride through Haarlem, Johns proceeds through a variety of transformations to arrive at the cast fragments of bodies which occupy the right-hand panel. The motifs of this and later pictures are very rarely determined by public symbols. Instead, they revolve around a personal response to the question of the relationship between the picture and reality. Johns exercised considerable influence on his generation and contributed to the emergence of both Minimal Art and Pattern Painting in the seventies. Without following directly in his footsteps, his fellow artists were deeply impressed by the consistency of his development from the fifties onwards.

By contrast, Rauschenberg expanded the concept 'picture' by his use of fragments of reality. He followed a path that had been pointed to by the late work of Kurt Schwitters. At the beginning of the fifties, he was already laying the foundations for the dominance of material in his 'combine paintings'.

Far-reaching experiments with white, or even silver-coloured paintings, with constructions made of cardboard and with cloth pictures marked out a wide area of artistic activity. At a very early stage, Rauschenberg's use of material found an echo in the cloth pictures of Alberto Burri, while his radical emptying of pictures coincided with the theories of Cy Twombly. The artist finally arrived at a solution by confronting clusters of abstract brushstrokes with concrete objects in order to make his pictures part of real space. At the same time, Rauschenberg developed a wide-ranging system of emblems. In *Odalisque* they exhibit manifold connections with the art of the past, while in *Axle* they conjure up the spirit of America in the sixties in the manner of a mural for a public building.

Johns and Rauschenberg, both of whom had maintained close ties with Paris from early on, opened up limitless possibilities for the real Pop Art generation. Thus, Claes Oldenburg was able to produce works which took sculpture to the verge of reality. With his first installations — for example, *The Street* — he adopted the coarse iconography and the poor materials of *Art brut,* before going on to create his first objects from the consumer world. Even in these works, he retained his claim to the status of a sculptor, as evinced by such masterful, apparently simple things as *White Shirt and Blue Tie* of 1961. Although everything in this work seems to be accommodated to the presenta- tion of a mere object, it was still the artist who created the sculpture out of plastic material and expressive colour. Oldenburg removes everyday objects so far from their normal context that the sculptures assert themselves as independent entities alongside reality, however close art and life seem to come.

The question concerning the boundary between a work of art and the viewer's space was posed in a striking way by the ensembles of figures with which George Segal confronted the beholder. Although the mood of the situations brings to mind scenes by Edward Hopper, Segal's use of plaster casts is reminiscent of death masks, while his surfaces recall Manzoni's *Achrome* and the tension between living bodies and the work of art in Yves Klein's *Anthropometry.* A work like Segal's *Woman Washing her Feet in a Sink* depicts in a disturbing fashion the loneliness of modern life, the isolation of the individual in society. Everyday situations are expanded into symbols of modern existence *per se.*

While these artists stood on the threshold between abstraction and a new approach to reality, there arose after 1960 a movement which not only opened up new paths to reality, but also concerned itself explicitly with the realities of modern life in the big city. The first steps towards Pop Art were taken by artists in London. Robert Kitaj, Peter Blake, Eduardo Paolozzi and Richard Hamilton transformed the visual manifestations of modern civilization, with its advertising, screen idols, newspapers and the like, into pictures which analysed and laid bare clichés of thinking and feeling. Hamilton's work realizes most convincingly the aim of elaborating on everyday triviality by means of quotations, photographs and reproductions. His art combines in a masterful way real things, photographs, half-tone prints, blots of colour, etc. to offer a critical view of *Trafalgar Square* or a commentary on the cult surrounding the filmstar Marilyn Monroe.

New York artists were concerned less with the iconographical methods of their London colleagues than with the growing fascination emanating from the mass media. Roy Lichtenstein pursued a radical dialogue with figure painting. His adaptation of the comic-strip provided a shock for 'High Art'. In an unheard-of manner, his compositions exposed, and at the same time accepted, aggression and sentimentality. Lichtenstein actually appeared to be using more or less unchanged originals as pictures. But from the outset, critics realized that the works harked back to the integra- tion of motif and picture plane contained in the late works of Léger and Matisse. *M-MAYBE* of 1965 exemplifies the extraordinary psychological concentration of Lichtenstein's work, as well as its perfect organization of the picture plane through the use of primary colours only, of clear lines and of a tight condensation of the original. Masterpieces of painting were thus created in the sixties which concerned themselves increasingly with 'art about art'. *Landscape with Figures and Rainbow* (1980), for example, alludes to the art of the Expressionists, while other works deal with Futurism and Art Deco. Apart from Lichtenstein, Andy Warhol also remained true to the style he had derived from the world of advertising and social clichés. He expunged from his works all traces of personal 'handwriting'. His paintings include trade marks, Pepsi-Cola advertisements or the photograph of a plane crash in such a way as to retain the icon-like quality of the originals. Around 1963, Warhol began to employ silk-screen printing as a means of transferring the images onto the canvas, thus granting his compositions greater variety. *Red Race Riot* of 1963 is a typical product of this style, reproducing photographs and removing them from their customary context with the aid of the silk-screen process. Transferring the motif onto canvas creates a seemingly arbitrary pictorial architecture which, like a film clip, lends the subject varying degrees of focus, density and presence in order to arrive at a hauntingly emblematic image.

Whereas Lichtenstein and Warhol understood Pop Art as the demise of subjectivity, of *peinture pure* and the artist's personal 'handwriting', James Rosenquist developed a kind of collage painting which showed a high level of technical refinement in terms of commercial art. His room installation *Horse Blinders* brings to a new peak the complex method of simulating collage technique with the help of fragments of realistic painting. The viewer of the work, which encompasses four walls of a room, is exposed to a whirling sequence of pieces of reality. Fragments of objects, cut-outs and details are mounted together to form a frieze in which the colours of one motif seem to melt into those of the next. In this work, which captures the beholder by surrounding him on all four sides, everything seems to be in a state of flux. The title *Horse Blinders* must be ironic, since the masterly painting within the confined field of vision offered by the enclosed space necessarily gives rise to a widening of associations and experience. Rosenquist's style of painting reflects the ideas of Duchamp: with no underlying narrative purpose, the constituents of the image collide in a seemingly unrelated way. On the other hand, Rosenquist points ahead to Chuck Close's photorealism which, in the work of Eric Fischl, finally linked up with American realism of the thirties.

Another group of important artists producing Pop Art made direct use of the sign-language of the big city. Robert Indiana may be regarded as a typical representative of this form of abstraction. Through the transformation of numbers and signs into pictorial objects, his style took on the clear disposition and shrill colour-signals of the original material. His version of Pop Art was a recurring factor in the critical reception accorded to this art in the sixties. Indiana's work seemed to have established an unequivocally modern iconography capable of matching the formal power of painting.

The impulses which emanated from Johns, Rauschenberg and Oldenburg at the end of the fifties had been transformed into a pictorial world that affirmed modern consumer society. It had left behind the formal and theoretical Dadaistic beginnings of American art in the sixties. Although links with European and earlier American art of the twentieth century – especially with Duchamp and his ideas – are quite apparent, the younger artists rejected Dada's criticism and denial of the concept 'picture'. Instead, they concentrated on its positive aspects, exploring the formal possibilities inherent in the transformation of ready-mades or in the tension between the picture and its meaning.

Pop Art bore an optimistic stamp. Its lighthearted, open view of modern civilization spread from America to the whole world, not least because it appeared to be endlessly reproducible. Art was shown how to expand its audience in a way that fascinated, and left its mark on, an entire generation.

135   Jasper Johns, *Untitled (Ale Cans),* 1960, Height 12 cm

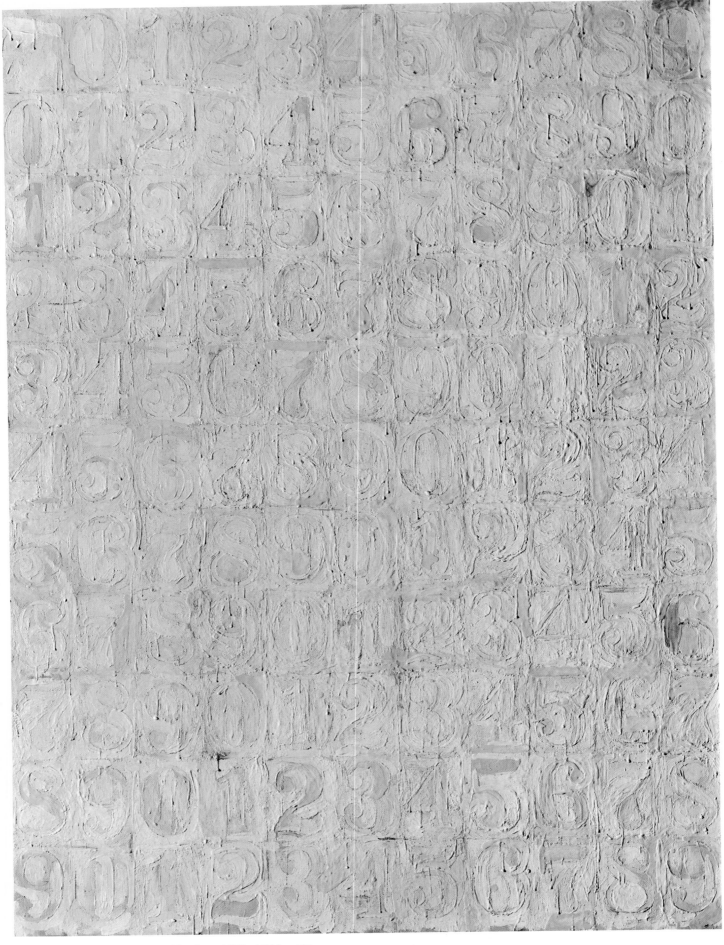

136   Jasper Johns, *Large White Numbers*, 1958, 170.5 × 126 cm

137   Jasper Johns, *Flag on Orange Field*, 1957, 167 × 124 cm

138   Jasper Johns, *Edingsville*, 1965, 173 × 311 cm

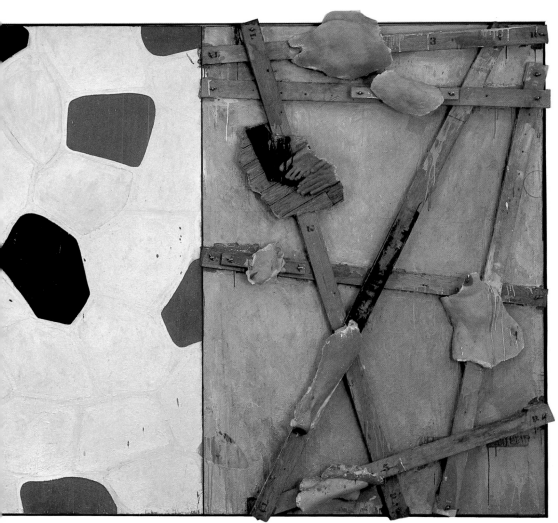

139   Jasper Johns, *Untitled*, 1972
183 × 490 cm

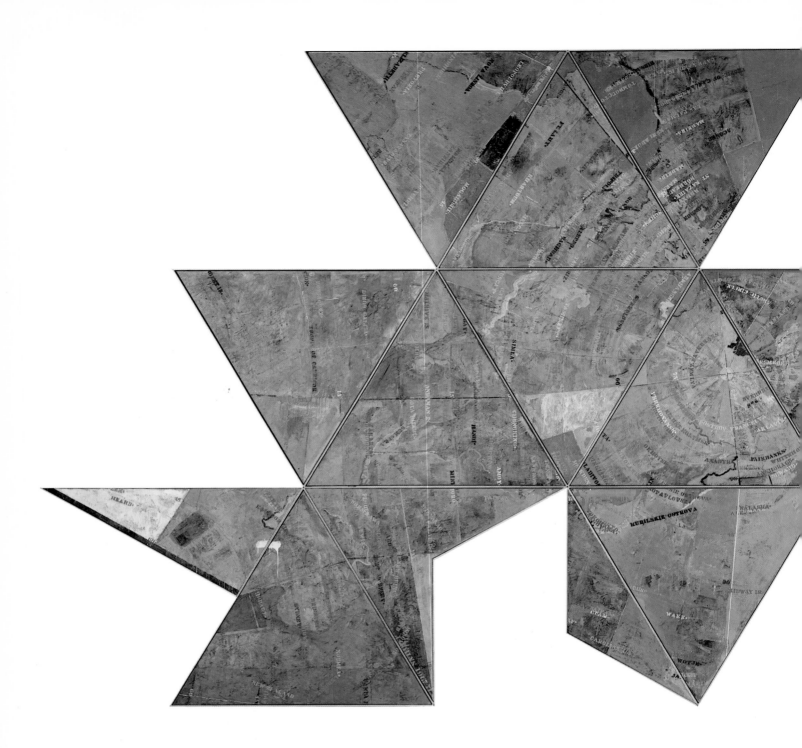

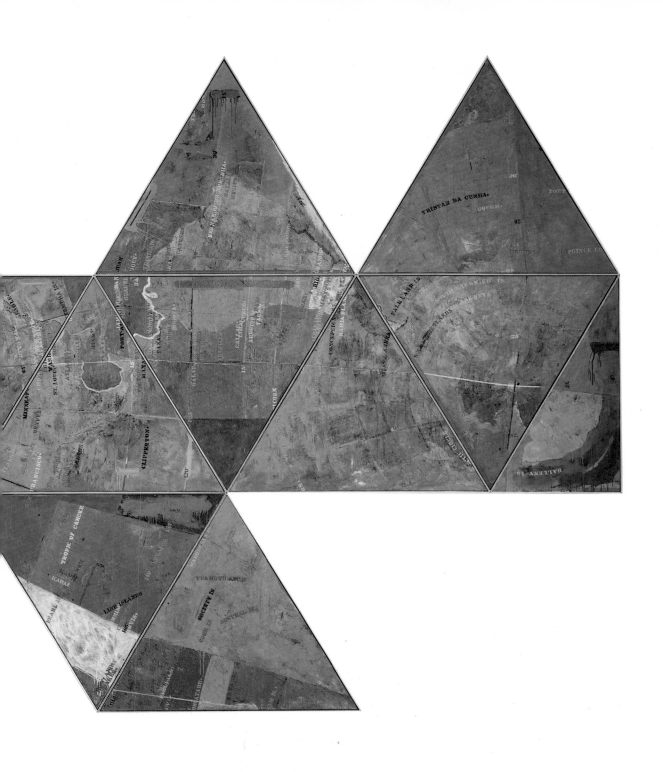

140   Jasper Johns, *Map*, 1967-71, 500 × 1,000 cm

141   Robert Rauschenberg, *Odalisque*
1955-58, 205 × 44 × 44 cm

142   Robert Rauschenberg
Black Market, 1961, 152 × 127 cm

143   Robert Rauschenberg, *Axle*, 1964, 274 × 610 cm

144   John Chamberlain, *White Shadow*, 1964, Height 172 cm

145   Andy Warhol, *Close Cover Before Striking – Pepsi-Cola*, 1962, 183 x 137 cm

146   Andy Warhol, *129 Die in Jet-Plane Crash*, 1962, 254.5 × 182.5 cm

147   Andy Warhol, *Red Race Riot*, 1963, 350 × 210 cm

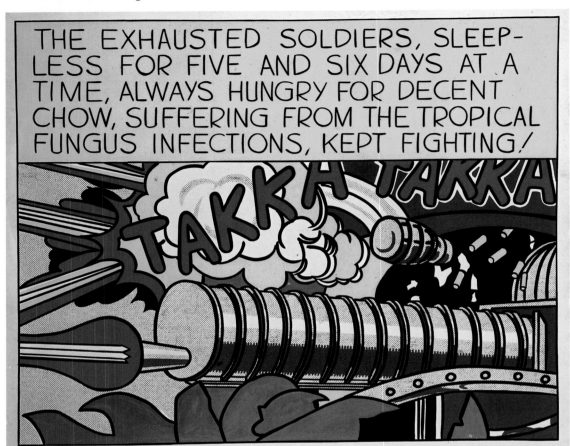

148   Roy Lichtenstein
Takka-Takka, 1962
142 × 173 cm

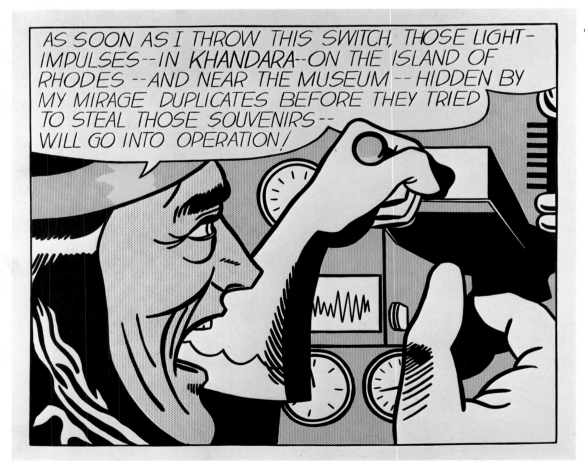

149   Roy Lichtenstein
Mad Scientist
1963, 127 × 151 cm

150   Roy Lichtenstein, *M-MAYBE (A Girl's Picture)*, 1965, 152 × 152 cm

151 Roy Lichtenstein, *Red Barn II*, 1969, 112 × 142 cm

152 Roy Lichtenstein, *Cloud and Sea*, 1964, 76 × 152.5 cm

153   Roy Lichtenstein, *Landscape with Figures and Rainbow*, 1980, 213 × 304.8 cm

154   Roy Lichtenstein, *Still Life with Net, Shell, Rope and Pulley*, 1972, 152 × 243.5 cm

155   Claes Oldenburg
Street Chick, 1960, 285 × 110 cm

156   Claes Oldenburg, *White Shirt
and Blue Tie,* 1961, 120 × 80 × 30 cm

157   Claes Oldenburg, *The Street*, 1960-84

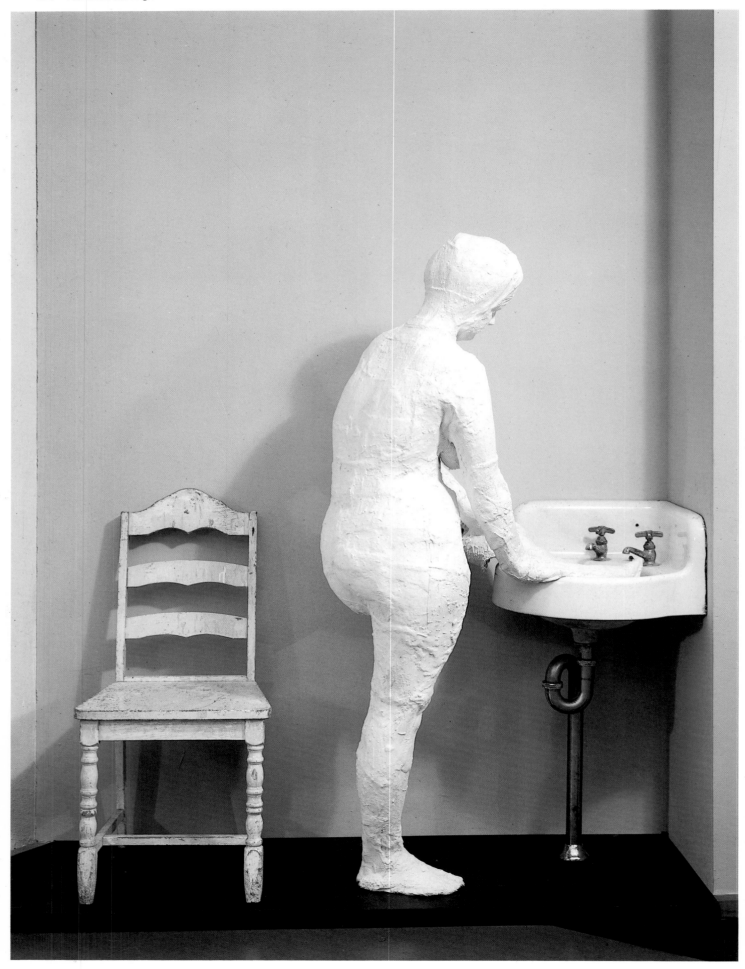

158   George Segal
Woman Washing her Feet in a Sink
1964/65, Height 152 cm

159   George Segal
The Restaurant Window, 1967
243 × 335 cm

160   Jim Dine, *Pleasure Palette*
1969, 152 × 102 cm

161   James Rosenquist
Horse Blinders (details), 1968/69, 275 × 2,530 cm

162   James Rosenquist, *Untitled (Joan Crawford says . . .)*, 1964, 242 × 196 cm

163   Robert Indiana, *USA 666 (Eat, Die, Err, Hug)*, 1966/67, 91.5 × 91.5 cm

164   Richard Lindner, *Disneyland*, 1965, 203 × 127 cm

165   Tom Wesselmann, *Bathtub 3*, 1963, 213 × 270 × 45 cm

166   Richard Hamilton, *Bathers I*, 1966/67, 84 × 117 cm

167   Richard Hamilton, *Trafalgar Square*, 1965-67, 80 x 120 cm

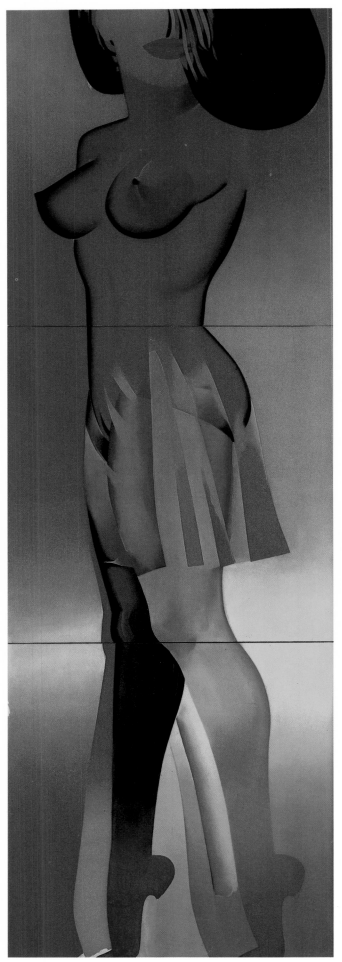

168   Allan Jones, *Perfect Match*
1966/67, 280 × 93 cm

169   Peter Blake, *ABC-Minors*, 1955, 72 x 46 cm

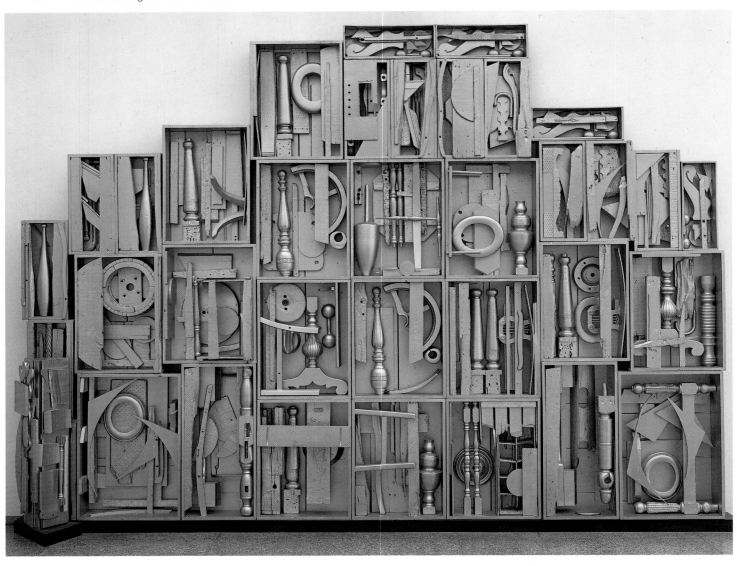

170   Louise Nevelson, *Royal Tide IV*, 1959/60, 335 x 427 cm

9

European Tendencies after 1945, II

The prognosis, often repeated in the years immediately after the war, that the future of the fine arts lay in abstraction was belied by the work being done at the time. Abstract art did indeed function as a symbol of freedom, especially in post-Fascist Germany. This, however, said little about the quality of the work being produced either in Germany, France or England. Significant new developments paid no heed to the belief in progress which accompanied the move from figurative to abstract art.

While many artists at this time used Surrealism as a means of reassessing their style, and usually arrived at a point far removed from it, Francis Bacon was to remain true to himself over a period of decades. What he created and repeatedly employed in his work was a realistic Surrealism that made use of the transformation of photographic impressions and of spaces which, in their perspective conception, radiated a sense of the unreal. Bacon sought, not a Surrealism of motifs, but one of painting itself, employing it to distort or blur the tangibly real motifs which made up his sorrowful universe. The uniqueness and peculiarity of Bacon's unswerving path from the 1930s onwards assured him the status of a lone wolf who, though barely classifiable, could not be ignored. Apart from Henry Moore, he was the only English artist to draw international attention to the wilful, individualistic native tradition. Bacon formulated the horror creatures have of their own vulnerability and inadequacy, creating metaphors for the threats to human existence posed by our century. He evoked most forcefully those moments of fear in human experience when reason seems to give way to insanity.

While Bacon incorporated himself, his portrait, his body and his situation, into his work, Jean Dubuffet was creating a pictorial world in Paris that transcended Surrealism in a quite different way. Dubuffet drew on sources of inspiration which he himself called 'art brut'. Children's drawings, the art of the mentally ill, graffitti and similar products of non-artists were all recognized by Dubuffet as means of achieving an unexpected intensity from the magical quality of simplicity.

The crisis in western thought following the Second World War is reflected in such a rejection of traditional artistic values in favour of a positive use of previously neglected cultural strata. *The Dog on the Table*, a painting dating from 1953, unites various elements of Dubuffet's development up to that year. He uses the palette-knife to create a relief-like mass of paint which lies like a light patch on the dark ground in a way reminiscent of Jean Fautrier's post-1940 pictures. As with Paul Klee (see, for example, *Highway and Byways* of 1929), impressed marks, drawings and letters of the alphabet are imprinted into the painted surface and constitute the real subject of the picture. The naive, childlike rendering of the objects, however, comes straight from *Art brut* and gives the painting that freshness and immediacy which Dubuffet found lacking in the art of his contemporaries. Despite changes of style, Dubuffet retained this concept throughout his work: it left its mark on the 'cellular style' of his *Hourloupe* cycle, on the *Portable Landscape* of 1968 and on the later *Activité généralisée*. Like 'Dada', 'Hourloupe' was a hybrid term, used to describe a style based on blue, black and red lines which bounded white, quasi-organic cells. A comparison of *The Dog on the Table* of 1953 and *Portable Landscape* of 1968 shows how consistent Dubuffet's motifs were, for without too much effort the landscape can also be seen as a table. The effect of the colours, however, varies considerably. The cells in *Hourloupe* overflow into three-dimensionality and help to create an artificial world which continually sets traps for the eye on the borderlines between volume, plane and space. The viewer is led away from an orientation towards customary reality into a blinding context of white which embraces him in another, separate reality.

Dubuffet's search for new sources of inspiration is typical of the art of that 'second avant-garde' which, in the half-decade following the war, laid the foundations for a new appraisal of aesthetic experience. Joseph Beuys, Lucio Fontana and Yves Klein certainly belong among these artists. Traces of Surrealism have virtually disappeared from their work. In its stead stands a common quest for the origins of art, a quest which is no longer based merely on formal simplification and reduction. As a reaction to the upheavals of the Second World War, these artists broke with the illusionistic aesthetics of the traditional picture in a quite radical way. Dubuffet had already begun to investigate the possibilites of sculpture. The crisis in painting as a representational and narrative medium had been exacerbated by Fascism's misuse of realistic art for propaganda purposes, so that an opening up of painting towards the use of relief, and even sculpture, became quite feasible. The content of such an art, based as it was on existentialist ideas, combined with crude and 'lowly' materials to produce works that undermined any middle-class notions of 'beauty'.

Beuys's work demonstrates in a unique way the transformation of modest, even ugly materials into magical works of art. He began where Schwitters had left off, incorporating the most insignificant-looking finds from nature into his assemblages. Over and above their formal innovations, *King's Daughter sees Iceland* and *Halved Felt Cross with Dust Picture 'Magda'*, both from 1960, are introductions to Beuys's thought. His complex iconography and pictorial language conjure up the contrasts in nature and in man as well as the historically based dichotomy in our ways of thinking (halved felt cross = schism Rome/Byzantium). Attempts to point out ways of overcoming these contradictions eventually led him into political activity.

With the employment of materials from everyday life, the concept of what exactly constitutes an image changed to such an extent that, in the end, the question of the relationship between life and art was raised. At that time, Beuys had in mind the supplanting of illusionism by a more open form of work which, like a holy relic, could produce an effect directly. With completely different means, Yves Klein and Lucio Fontana were addressing the same problem, and the result of all these efforts was the dissolution and transcending of existentialist individualism. A way out of the isolation of the individual was sought by Beuys in terms of 'energy', by Klein in the idea of monochrome brilliance of colour and by Fontana in his *concetto spaziale* ('spatial concept').

Yves Klein's ideas broke the passive self-sufficiency of the traditional picture in order to restructure both the relationship between the artist and his work and that between the work and its beholder. Klein was able to orchestrate the effectiveness of his pictures without actually becoming a painter in the customary sense. His blue paint, carefully selected and mixed with the help of a chemist, had its own transcendental aura. He employed fire or naked bodies covered in paint to leave marks on the picture surface and soaked sponges in pigment in order to make the paint itself a three-dimensional body.

By contrast, Fontana perforated and cut up his canvases in order to make space itself visible. His attacks on the concept 'picture' opened up a limitless freedom for concrete art. As with Yves Klein, the rejection of representational space gave rise to an evocation of materiality which acquired great poetic force through the traces left by the artist in his work. Seen from this vantage point, the early *Harlequin* and *Columbine* seem at first sight to be condensations of Baroque figures. Yet the characterization of their movements, and the way the shaping of the figures is halted at the required moment, already show Fontana's treatment of material to be leading in new directions. The coloured glaze of the figures suggests a duality of painting and sculpture which was to remain the subject of all Fontana's subsequent work.

Taking the self as their starting point, these artists arrived at a formulation of being and existence which was founded in the individual's power of imagination. Just a few years later, this equivalence of art and life, this romantic idea of a oneness of thought and feeling, was to be realized in a much more direct manner. All three artists mentioned were at pains to provide a philosophical, theoretical basis for their approach, which attempted to deal with the tension between life and art by means of premeditated images. The synthetic core of the pictorial language of Beuys, Fontana and Klein deserves special mention in order to emphasize the difference between these works and those later ones which incorporated real surroundings directly.

In 1961 the New Realists put on their first group exhibition in Paris. Besides Klein, the movement included such artists as Daniel Spoerri, Christo, Arman, Hains, Villéglé, Dufrêne, Deschamps, Tinguely and the Italian Rotella. The most important inspiration came from Marcel Duchamp, who was also being discovered as a father of modern art in New York at about the same time. His idea of the ready-made proved to be exceptionally fruitful for those wishing to operate in the undefined area between art and reality. Spoerri applied Duchamp's ideas in a radical fashion in his 'trap pictures', which were created from the remains of gatherings or meals. *Robert's Table* originated during a conversation with Filliou. At a particular moment, dicided by Spoerri, the table and its contents were fixed in place and turned into a work of art by being hung on the wall.

Like Pop Art, Nouveau Réalisme, as the movement was christened by its theoretician and critic Pierre Restany, concerned itself with the typical phenomena of modern life in the big city. Décollage and assemblage were employed to include such elements of modern civilization as posters and objects from everyday life as guarantors of a new realism. In this way, the artists also dealt with the myths and dreams associated with the cinema. The artistic effect of torn-off and partially covered posters had already been recognized and recorded in photographs by Wols in the 1930s. Around 1960, the 'Décollagistes' in Paris sought to oppose Art informel with carefully composed images which, in the manner of Duchamp, emphasized the nature of the work as an object. Nevertheless, the poster fragments were still governed by an abstract pictorial language. The other method of the New Realists, assemblage, had already been used by the Dadaists to combat the traditional substance of sculpture. In an apparently random fashion, Arman piled together relics of everyday life to form tableaux which, in the sixties, often contained only one particular kind of object — milk-cans, for example. Arman himself spoke of these works as 'accumulations'. He provided them with visual unity by arranging the identical objects in rows or recurring patterns.

Jean Tinguely's works do not fit entirely into the 'assemblage' category, since movement and sound are a part of their conception. Tinguely created perfect, yet absurd, apparatuses out of machine parts, wheels, springs, bells and the like. As in *Balouba no. 3*, the machines serve no particular purpose, but simply move senselessly and incomprehensibly in a random stuttering rhythm. This is to be understood as an ironic comment on the worship of all things technical in the modern age. The title *Balouba* alludes to an African tribe whose ritual dance seems to be being performed by this monster. With his intentional misunderstanding of mechanical processes, the artist interprets ready-made art in a new way. But he also refers ironically to the art of Constructivists like Gabo and Pevsner by carrying their plastic conception of space to absurd extremes.

The European trends which appeared as parallels to neo-Dada and Pop Art in the United States certainly did not interpret the world in such a positive way as the American movements. Duchamp was an important point of departure for artists on both sides of the Atlantic, but they drew different conclusions from his work. Despite such cooperation as that within the Fluxus movement, the art of each continent obeyed its own laws and followed its own path.

171   Francis Bacon, *Painting 1946, Second version*, 1971, 198 × 147 cm

172   Jean Dubuffet, *The Dog on the Table,* 1953, 89.7 × 116.5 cm

173   Jean Dubuffet, *Portable Landscape,* 1968, 100 × 140 × 100 cm

174   Jean Dubuffet, *Activité généralisée (no. 14)*, 1976, 221 x 249 cm

175   Antoni Tàpies, *Large Black and brown Craquelé*, 1966, 260 x 195 cm

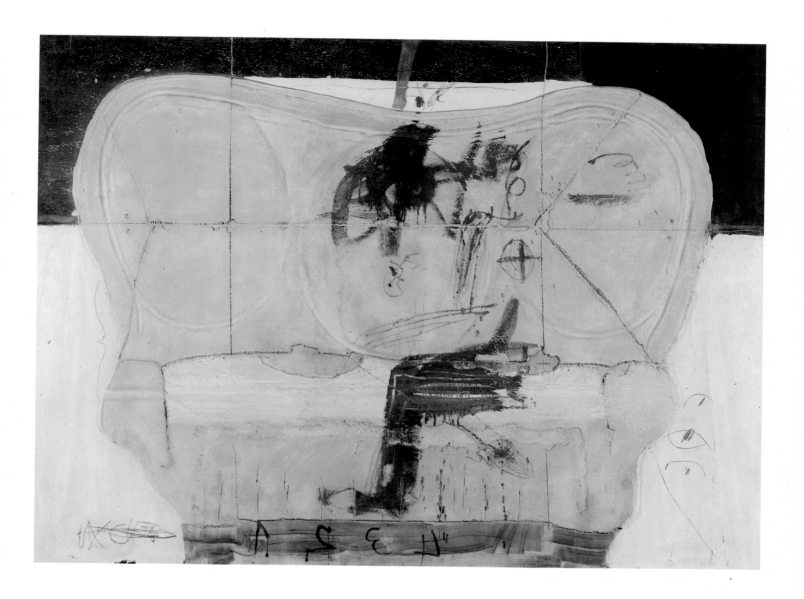

176   Antoni Tàpies, *Signs on White Ovals*, 1966, 196 × 260 cm

177   Lucio Fontana, *Columbine,* 1949, Height 55 cm

178 Lucio Fontana, *Harlequin*, 1949, Height 55.5 cm

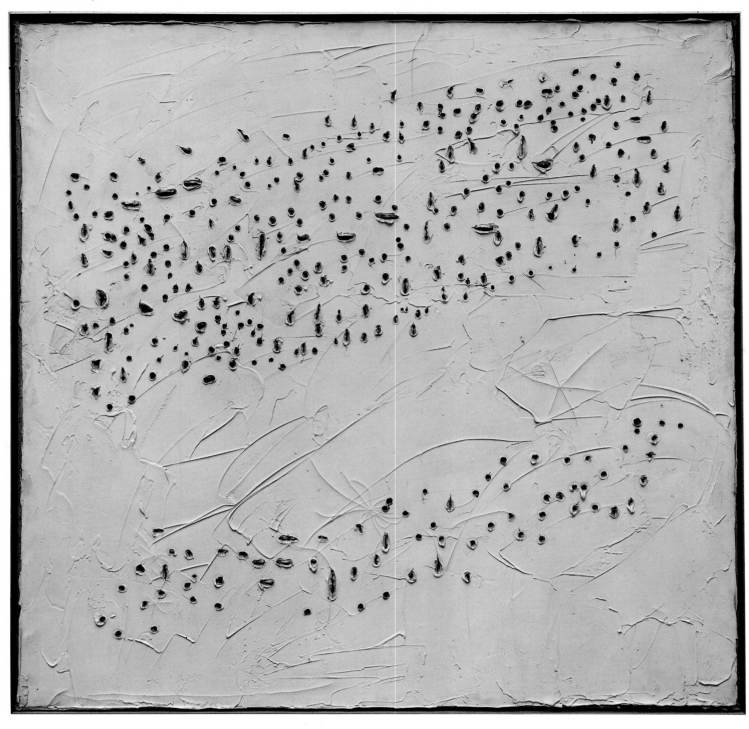

179   Lucio Fontana, *Spacial Concept:*
Marriage in Venice, 1960/61, 152 × 154 cm

180   Lucio Fontana
Spatial Sculpture, 1957,
Height 150 cm

181   Yves Klein, *Anthropometry: ANT 130*, 1958, 194 × 127 cm   182   Yves Klein, *Blue Sponge Relief: RE 19*, 1958, 200 × 165 cm

183   Joseph Beuys
King's Daughter sees Iceland
1960, 114 × 99 cm

184   Joseph Beuys
Halved Felt Cross with Dust Picture
'Magda', 1960, 108 × 68 cm

185   Joseph Beuys, *Sibyl (Justice)*, 1957, 24 × 50 × 185 cm

186   Joseph Beuys, *Double Aggregate*, 1959 (1969), 108 × 314 × 78.5 cm

187   Arnulf Rainer, *Violet Vertical*, 1961, 200 × 130 cm

188   Daniel Spoerri
Robert's Table, 1961, 200 × 50 cm

189   Jean Tinguely
Balouba no. 3, 1959, Height 144 cm

190   Mimmo Rotella, *Cinemascope*, 1962, 173 × 133 cm

191   Arman, *Accumulation of Milk-cans*, 1961, 83 × 140 × 40 cm

192   Arman, *Poubelle no. 1*, 1960, 52 × 71.5 × 13 cm

193   Renato Guttuso, *Caffè Greco*, 1976, 182 × 333 cm

10

Forms of Realism

The style of Realism stood at the very beginning of modern art. Around the middle of the nineteenth century, Courbet had introduced the term as a slogan directed against Romantic and Neoclassical orthodoxies, thereby starting a process which, paradoxically, was to end in the pronounced non-realism of Cubism.

Realism returned in various forms after the First World War. *Neue Sachlichkeit* ('New Objectivity'), Verism and *Valori plastici* ('Plastic Values') all describe artistic movements that became increasingly successful at breaking through the strategies of the avant-garde. Under Fascist governments, Realism was perverted into a propaganda art which also made use of a polished veneer of classicism. Realism had already become the basic style of American painting in the nineteenth century. From Winslow Homer to Thomas Eakins and Edward Hopper, America produced a large number of important Realists who, especially in the 1930s, concerned themselves with social themes.

This connection between art and social emancipation also took effect in Europe when, in *Guernica,* Picasso used the means of modern art in an attempt to create a history painting based on a significant contemporary event. After the war, he influenced numerous politically minded artists in both East and West. As a result of his study of Picasso's wartime work, Renato Guttuso arrived at a form of Realism which, extended by the use of stylistic 'quotations', gained a new dimension of complexity.

The various qualities of Guttuso's painting are combined in the late *Caffè Greco,* in which masterly adaptations of diverse motifs are united by the artist's sovereign compositional skill. Reality and memory intermingle here. Just as the collection of people in the famous artists' café in Rome includes both contemporaries and such notable figures from the past as de Chirico and Buffalo Bill, so 'quotations' from the art of Antiquity or from Picasso are integrated into the composition as a whole. From 1977 onwards, Jörg Immendorff was inspired to reply to Guttuso in his *Café Deutschland* pictures.

Following the magnificent abstract painting produced after 1940, and the revival of Duchamp's ideas, Realism in America was taken up again parallel to Conceptual Art. The depiction of a *Foodshop* by Richard Estes demonstrates the approach of this new Realism, which makes use of photography while going far beyond it. Recording details with even greater meticulousness than the camera, the painter adds to the exactitude of the original photograph an omnipresent sense of detail, achieved by impressively sophisticated means. Various reflections are superimposed on one another in order to arrive at a type of concentrated cipher of reality which is beyond the reach of the camera.

Alex Colville's painting makes plain to an even greater degree the subtle control exerted by the Photorealists in their pictures. A work like *Truck Stop* was prepared with the utmost care by means of construction drawings, studies of proportion and the like. This almost symbolic justification for each and every part of the composition lends a special dignity and solemnity to the end product.

By perfecting the techniques of realistic painting, these artists completely exclude the element of fortuity inherent in photography. Although the view presented is partial, these condensed, icon-like images do offer a valid picture of America. The extreme realism of Photorealism is equally arresting in three dimensions. With Duane Hanson's *Woman with a Purse* or John de Andrea's *Studio Scene* an astounding, even frightening, reality enters the world of art. The distinction between art and reality appears to have been abolished quite ruthlessly, as the category 'sculpture' is replaced by a *trompe-l'œil* effect which, at first sight, the eye cannot cope with in these terms. In contrast to this deceptive reproduction of reality, the works of George Segal use the technique of alienation, the figures being encased in the stiff numbness of white plaster.

One of the masterpieces of realist sculpture from post-war America is Edward Kienholz's *Portable War-memorial.* Although employing a drastic verism, Kienholz goes beyond this by creating a greater density of form and content through the complex use of assemblage and 'quotation' techniques. The 'memorial' takes as its point of departure the well-known photograph from the war against Japan, in which American soldiers are shown raising the stars and stripes over the Pacific island of Iwo-Jima on the morning of 23 February 1945. The picture became very popular as a symbol of military heroism. It is at this point that Kienholz intervenes. The narrative of his monumental tableau runs from left to right. An enlistment poster and the patriotic singer Kate Smith in a barrel stand at the beginning of military life. In the middle are the names of 475 countries, once independent, which disappeared or received new borders as a result of war. Space is left for further names in order to make clear that the terrible history of human aggression is not a thing of the past but is being continued daily. Such a warning monument can therefore be taken to any and every place in the world, as the title suggests. The group of flag-raising soldiers from the photograph bursts frighteningly into the restaurant scene occupying the middle and right side of the monument, providing the consumer society with a shocking 'memento'. The viewer – or user – of the work of art is drawn into this world of horror, frozen in silver: the Coca Cola machine functions as usual and Kate Smith can still be heard bawling out her song. Kienholz gives back to Realism that moral dimension which had contributed so substantially to its birth in the middle of the nineteenth century. Free of ideological bias, his work is that of a critically aware contemporary.

194   Malcolm Morley, *St. John's Yellow Pages*, 1971, 159 × 137 cm

195   Richard Estes, *Foodshop*, 1967, 166 × 123.5 cm

196   Alex Colville, *Truck Stop*, 1966, 91.6 × 91.6 cm

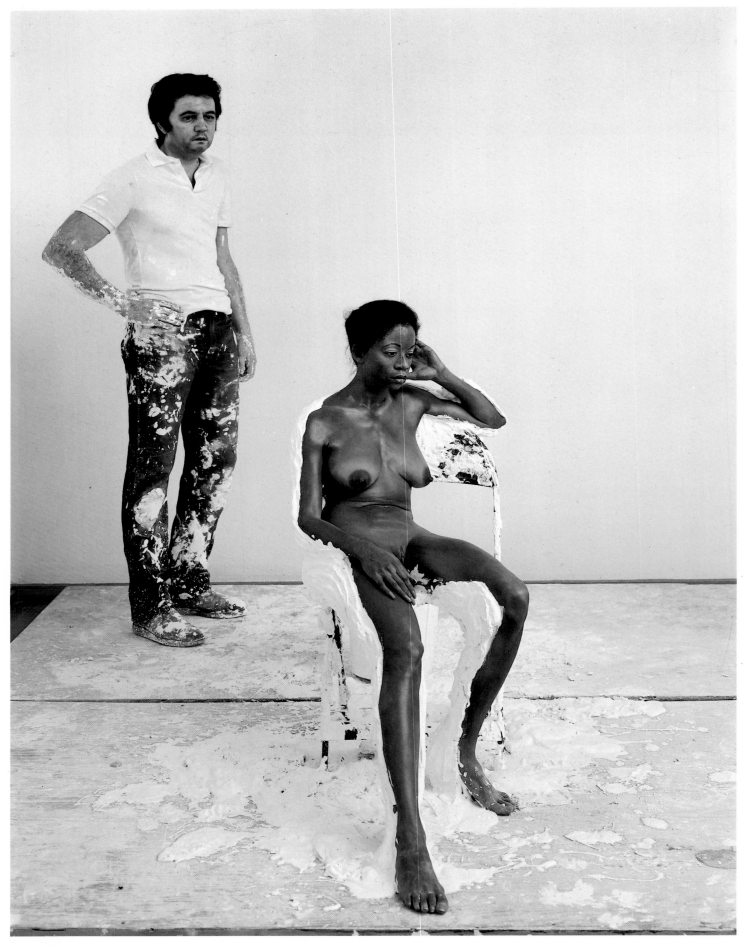

197   John de Andrea, *Untitled (Studio Scene)*, 1977, Height 185 and 115 cm

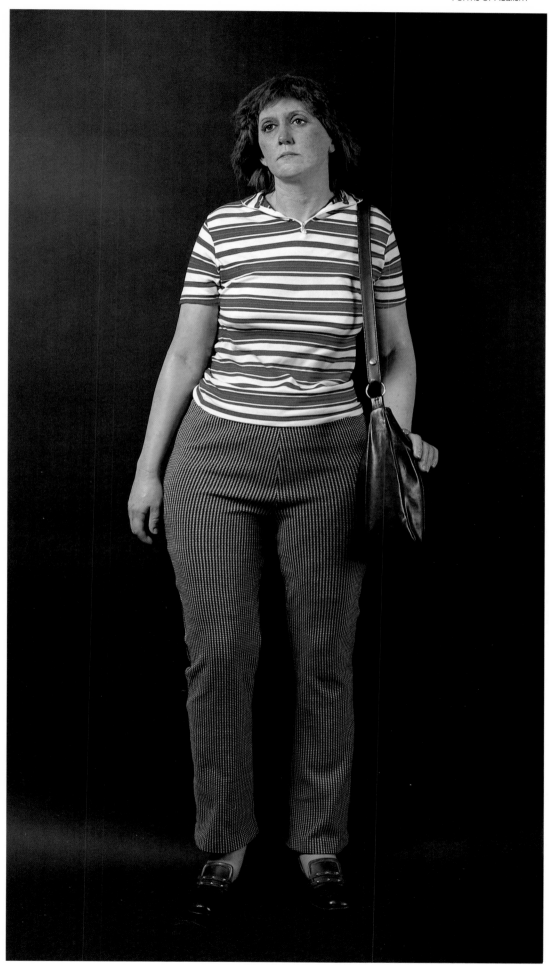

198 Duane Hanson
Woman with a Purse, 1974
Height 163 cm

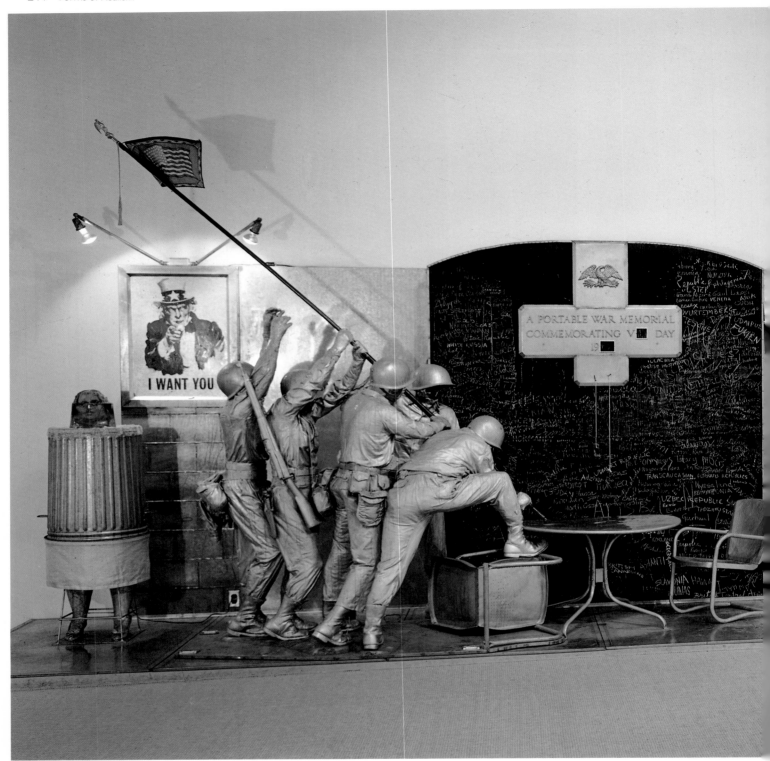

199   Edward Kienholz,   *The Portable War-memorial*, 1968, 285 × 950 × 240 cm

200   Franz Gertsch, *Marina making up Luciano*, 1975, 234 × 346.5 cm

II

German Art since 1960

The history of modern art in Germany was more strongly determined by external interference than by those inner laws which usually govern developments in the visual arts. As the capital of the united Germany which followed on the Franco-Prussian War of 1870-71, Berlin might have expected to acquire an avant-garde appropriate to its new status. Yet before such an avant-garde could establish itself, a conservative reaction set in under Wilhelm II which forced progressive elements into isolation and even led to the dismissal of forward-looking museum directors. An official art of pompous realism in the style of Anton von Werner set the tone. On top of this, only a few years remained for the German avant-garde to break new ground before the outbreak of the First World War, and by 1918 some of its best artists had fallen or had had their spirit broken by the experience of war. At the beginning of the Weimar Republic, German art was thus faced with another new beginning, one marked above all by the foundation of the Bauhaus. Yet such promising developments in a period of political confusion were soon brought to an end in 1933, when the enforced dictates of national optimism and realism routed the avant-garde. Many artists left the country, while others reacted by withdrawing from public life into 'inner emigration'. The utopia of modern art was a lost cause.

Following a few years of hesitation after 1945, the only feasible way forward seemed to lay in the adoption of, and adaptation to, the doctrines currently in vogue in East and West. The western part of the country chose abstraction, the 'free' style. Not having passed through the necessary historical process of growth and analysis, the post-war generation found itself with the vocabulary but not the grammar of abstract art – it had at first little direction of its own. A few exceptions stood out above the flood of abstract conformity, but it was not until the end of the 1950s that a renewed awareness of the problems inherent in Germany's own traditions began to make itself felt. At an early stage, Joseph Beuys had taken up a stand against informal abstraction, without, however, receiving any public approval or even notice. Apart from him, it was Georg Baselitz in Berlin who, around 1960, manifested a will to go his own stylistic way. The exhibition of his *Great Night Down the Drain* and *Naked Man* in 1963 led to a scandal, and the works were confiscated. With these pictures, Baselitz vehemently opposed non-commital, decorative art and, on behalf of himself and other artists, touched upon the wounds of history and the rootless situation of artists in the new German society. He found his first ally in Ralf Winkler from Dresden, who later adopted the name of the geologist and researcher into the ice age, Albrecht Penck. Nevertheless, it took until about 1980 before a broader debate set in which, with the presentation of Baselitz's first sculpture at the Venice Biennale, increased in vehemence. It was Baselitz's idea to regain the emotionality of painting on the basis of a non-narrative, abstract pictorial concept which might also be used as a weapon against aesthetic indifference.

What Baselitz attempted to achieve with individual pictorial means, Penck sought to work out systematically in his 'world pictures'. His analysis continually referred to the complete field of interaction between the individual and the system, as he knew it from the realities of a state like East Germany. Penck concerned himself, not only with Baselitz, but also with Beuys's concept of art, which also attempted a holistic explanation of art and life in which every detail had its place. Penck devised all kinds of situations for a relationship between the individual and the system, using cardboard models to simulate them in a simple but impressive way. At the beginning of the seventies, he worked serially and conceptually on the solution of artistic problems through a reduction of everything to the basic categories of perception and thought. As ever, Penck was concerned, not with eliminating the self from the artistic process, but rather with analysing the position of the self by means of an artistic process which was systematic. The subject of the search presented in *World Picture* of 1965 still dominates his work around 1970, though the means employed are less romantic. Penck has retained from his early work a cipher-like style of figure which recalls Klee and the exponents of *Art brut*. As late as 1983, a large-scale picture like *Standart VI* is dominated by a figure reduced to a few lines and surrounded by explanatory attributes giving rise to various associations. Penck's art moves in the realm of the borderline between figure and concept. It finds poetic metaphors for the problems to which the modern individual is exposed, without forgetting that in every situation that individual is under constant threat and attack.

Palermo (i. e. Peter Heisterkamp) also started out from realistic painting, before the influence of Beuys led him towards a glowing, emotional abstraction, the qualities of which had already become apparent before his death at the early age of thirty-four. Contact with New York during his last years resulted in greater concentration and severity, achieved by a fine balancing of the proportions of colour fields. *Directions I* of 1976 is created from an unpretentious collection of geometric stripes which, uniting to form a floating, elegant harmony, give expression to variations in direction. By applying the paint to sheets of metal instead of canvas, Palermo produces a strong material quality which increases the radiance of the colour even on this small scale.

In addition to Beuys and Palermo, the post–1960 avant-garde in the Rhineland received important impulses from Gerhard Richter and Sigmar Polke. Photographs provided Richter with the motifs of his pictures. This explains why his early work was deemed a German variant of Pop Art, a characterization which misinterprets the artist's intentions. With but few exceptions, his subjects did not come from the world of popular culture, neither was it his aim to utilize that world's images as a means of affirming traditional concepts of the picture. Rather, he was seeking a style which, through the use of blurring glazes of colour, would literally separate the painting from its motif.

This painter's scrupulous intellectual investigation of his métier was governed by the Protestant tradition of questioning the *raison d'être* of images. This is confirmed explicitly by the picture *Ema,* which takes its inspiration from the epoch-making *Nude Descending a Staircase* by that great doubter and heretic of modern art, Marcel Duchamp.

The subsequent breaks in the continuity of Richter's work have led in recent years to abstract pictures which condense models from informal abstraction, granting them an evocative reality through the effective shaping of the picture surface. Grooves, streaks and layered strokes of colour give rise to spaces which may be construed as worlds in themselves. As such, they are part of this artist's pre-occupation with visible reality, the representability of which he has repeatedly questioned.

Like Richter, Sigmar Polke appeared to come close to Pop Art during the sixties, using newspaper pictures, photographs, images from advertising and the technique of photogravure printing at a time when Roy Lichtenstein was doing the same thing in New York. However, Polke often derived his motifs and style, not from the world around him, but from that of the 1950s in an attempt to create indirect links with the aesthetics of pre-war Germany.

Polke investigated and expanded the technical possibilities of modern painting in a sovereign manner. Like an alchemist, he employed varnishes, mineral-based materials, pigments, metals, etc. in order to redefine the substance of pictures. In doing so, Polke did not act as a painter in the traditional sense, but rather as a manager, directing the ingredients of a work. A picture's materials contribute decisively to its existence, and may even give birth to its iconography. Polke grants fortuity a share in the paths taken by his imagination. He worked out numerous strategies for transforming matter into pictorial substance and for transposing ideas into the material form of a picture. These various approaches have opened up almost limitless possibilities for a younger generation of artists.

By taking pictorial structures to daring extremes, Polke has exceeded the present limits of painting in a critically constructive way. On the other hand, a pictorial magic shimmers through the complex fabric of materials and motifs, and this recalls Joseph Beuys's conception of art.

The extraordinary variety of new contributions made by German artists since 1960, the productive dialogue with the international avant-garde, the wide spectrum of approaches and the great number of significant works have combined to make the last twenty-five years one of the most fruitful and important epochs in the history of German art since Expressionism.

The work of Anselm Kiefer also took as its point of departure the materiality of Baselitz's early pictures. *Tree with Wing* (1973) adopts the earth colours of the early Baselitz. However, Kiefer interprets the use of impasto in terms of content, the relief produced by the application of paint realizing in a very direct way the pictorial concept first developed by Baselitz. In Kiefer's early work, the cleft between pictorial space and picture plane is extreme. By the early seventies, he had succeeded in creating a relief-like painted surface which approached the textures of Abstract

Expressionism. *Tree with Wing* shows Kiefer employing a speculative, poetic use of the space between the bark-like layers of paint and the lead wing in order to suspend the realism of the painting and set in motion those extraordinary powers of association which constitute the special quality of his pictorial language.

At the start of their careers, both Kiefer and Penck were affected by Beuys, who must rank as one of the seminal influences on German post-war art. Markus Lüpertz, too, spent a short time at the Düsseldorf Academy of Art, before arriving at his own type of picture, which he developed from the idea of 'dithyrambic painting'. Lüpertz represents the type of artist who reflects in an aggressive way on his own attitudes and the role of the artist in modern society. Like Picabia, he makes deliberate use of stylistic discords as a means of emphasizing the non-conformity of his work, a strategy which reached a climax in the 'German motifs' of around 1970. The huge-scale *Sinking Helmets* combines all the salient features of Lüpertz's art. It transforms an object highly charged with negative emotions – the helmet of the German *Wehrmacht* – into an artistic metaphor which goes so far as to reveal the essential head-shape underlying the helmet. The helmet becomes an allegory of the human head, which can be interpreted both as death and as a symbol of power. The noticeably gentle, almost fluid painting stands in complete contrast to the emphatically sculptural motifs, with their singularly dynamic interaction of opulent form and hollow body. By adding the quasi-medieval motif of stars on a red ground, the artist transposes the contents of the picture onto a plane which recalls the solemn solidity of sculpted Romanesque capitals. The expressive force derived from an artistic transcending of given materials also proves decisive in the sculpture *Titan,* made in 1983. Lüpertz draws on antique sculpture, animating its gestures and power, not by reproducing the action or motifs, but by using his own style in order to condense it into an image of impressive boldness.

Although hardly any connections exist between Lüpertz and Jörg Immendorff on a stylistic level, the work of both is concerned with the individual experience of the artist himself. Immendorff investigated the artistic claims of Beuys in order to arrive at his own pictorial language. He very consciously reflected on the crisis which had befallen representational art as a result of the social disturbances of 1968. Rejecting blind iconoclasm even at that date, he was convinced that art has a part to play in times of social upheaval. Beuys, of course, shared this conviction and, despite certain reservations, believed in the concrete effectiveness of art. Earlier on in the sixties, Immendorff had already become involved in the debate about realism in painting, i.e. about the latter's potential for effecting change. He reinterpreted Beuys's conceptualization of the problem, projecting it in 1977-78 onto the concrete historical situation of a divided Germany. Immendorff's realism never disavowed its origins in conceptual theory. *Café Deutschland,* a subject he has returned to since 1978, was indeed a place of his imagining, although it is full of symbols treated in a concrete manner. In fact, Immendorff gave the most direct expression to the problem of Germany, to the question of where exactly this divided nation stands in the conflict between East and West. Beuys had dealt with the theme in a cryptic way – through his symbol of the divided cross, for example – but Immendorff approaches political reality directly. In doing so, he was inspired by Guttuso's *Caffè Greco,* which displays a view of reality that Immendorff wished to grant new force. The fascinating chain of motifs and symbols set free by Immendorff in his treatment of the subject 'Germany' culminated in the monumental sculpture *Brandenburg Gate – World Question,* which was first shown at the Documenta 7 exhibition in 1984. Immendorff's early work had shown pronounced sculptural tendencies, and in this piece they are condensed into a monument which gives the 'German question' an existential dimension through the impressive use of symbolic objects.

201   Georg Baselitz, *The Great Night Down the Drain*, 1962/63, 250 × 180 cm

202 Georg Baselitz, *Pastoral (The Night)*
1985/86, 330 × 330 cm

203 Georg Baselitz, *Model for
a Sculpture,* 1980, 210 × 240 × 50 cm

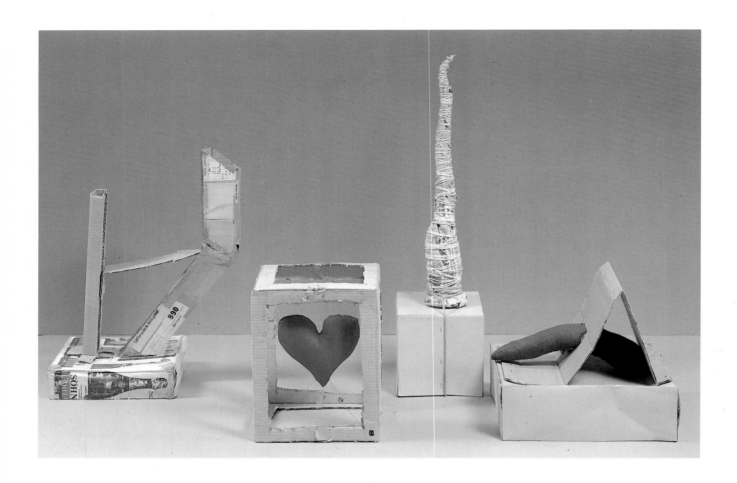

204   A. R. Penck, *Standart Models*, 1973/74

205   A. R. Penck, *World Picture*, 1965,   180 × 260 cm

206   A. R. Penck, *Standart VI*, 1983, 350 × 260 cm

207   Anselm Kiefer, *Tree with Wing*, 1979, 285 × 190 cm

208   Markus Lüpertz, *Titan*
1985, Height 253 cm

209   Markus Lüpertz
Summer's Day, 1985, 270 × 400 cm

210   Markus Lüpertz, *Sinking Helmets (dithyrambic I)*, 1970, 260 × 450 cm

211   Jörg Immendorff, *Café Deutschland 1*, 1977/78, 282 × 320 cm

212   Blinky Palermo, *Directions I*, 1976, 26.7 × 21 cm each

213   Gerhard Richter
Abstract no. 559/2, 1984, 200 × 300 cm

214   Gerhard Richter, *Ema –*
Nude on the Stairs, 1966, 200 × 130 cm

215   Sigmar Polke, *Envy and Avarice*, 1984, 261 x 200 cm

216   Antonius Höckelmann
Trial Hop with Die, 1974
320 × 130 cm

Alphabetical list of the artists and their works

(The numbers refer to the colour plates)